MEETING SPECIAL NEEDS IN THE EARLY YEARS

Directions in Policy and Practice

Edited by
Sheila Wolfendale

David Fulton Publishers
London

David Fulton Publishers Ltd
The Chiswick Centre, 414 Chiswick High Road, London W4 5TF
www.fultonpublishers.co.uk

First published in Great Britain in 1997 by David Fulton Publishers

Note: The right of Sheila Wolfendale to be identified as the author of this work
have been asserted by her in accordance with the Copyright, Designs and
Patents
Act 1988.

David Fulton Publishers is a division of Granada Learning Limited, part of
Granada plc.

Copyright © David Fulton Publishers

British Library Cataloguing in Publication Data
A catalogue record for this book is available from the British Library.

ISBN 1-85346-453-8

Typeset by FSH Limited, London
Printed and bound in Great Britain

Contents

Contributors

Fiona Barnett, Loraine Hancock, Julia Hardy and **Marianne McCarthy** at the time of writing were educational psychologists working for Hammersmith and Fulham LEA. Prior to becoming educational psychologists all four authors were qualified teachers working in a range of schools, across the age range. Fiona now works in Essex LEA as an educational psychologist; Julia now works in Lambeth as Principal Educational Psychologist.

Mary Burke has been the London Borough of Hackney's Peripatetic Teacher for the Visually Impaired since 1987. Before this she worked for many years in a special school for the visually impaired in Inner London. As well as working with children and their parents, her work brings her into wide-ranging contact with educational, health and social services professionals.

Moira Challen is a senior educational psychologist in the London Borough of Barking and Dagenham with special responsibility for Early Years Coordination and Professional Development. She previously worked as a psychologist in the London Borough of Havering. Her teaching experience was with secondary aged pupils and special needs pupils across the age range.

Lesley Fleming is an educational psychologist employed by Surrey County Council. She previously worked as an educational psychologist in the London Borough of Wandsworth where she had an under-fives responsibility. She has experience in teaching primary aged pupils with language impairments. She currently supports two specialist language units in Surrey.

Mark Fox worked as an educational psychologist in Solihull, and later in Bromley, where he was in charge of the School Psychological service. He then had a combined post for Professional Development in Essex LEA and as a tutor for Advanced and Initial Training for EPs at the University of East London. He is presently Head of the Advisory Assessment Service at SCOPE. He has a particular interest in working with preschool children and their families and with children with severe and complex difficulties.

Jo Goodall is currently working part-time for BAECE (British Association for Early Childhood Education) as a National Field Officer and as an independent early years consultant and inspector. She has experience in working in a range of early years environments and in particular with children with special educational needs. Her previous post was as County Adviser for Early Years in Essex where she is now an Education Associate.

Ellen Guerin recently qualified as an educational psychologist from Nottingham University. She is currently working for the London Borough of Tower Hamlets Educational Psychology Service. She qualified as a primary school teacher in Ireland and worked in Inner London schools. To date, Ellen has been involved in a borough-wide Portage in Nurseries project and research into the suitability of Phonological Awareness testing for bilingual pupils.

Cathy Hamer is an experienced early years teacher and senior educational psychologist. In 1989 Cathy became Portage Supervisor and was responsible for developing links with the Child Development Centre, leading to a unified Preschool Service of which she is now Head.

Karen Hobson is a senior educational psychologist (acting) with the London Borough of Redbridge Educational Psychology Service. Her current post involves managing educational support services for preschool children and liaison with health and social services. Prior to becoming an educational psychologist, Karen was a teacher at a special school in Essex for pupils with emotional and behavioural needs. Her current professional areas of interest include promoting children's self-esteem, collaborative assessments with parents and in-service training for teachers in schools.

Dr Chris Lloyd is senior lecturer responsible for special educational needs in the School of Education at the University of Greenwich. She teaches on programmes of study for practising teachers, including MA, BA/BSc and DPSE routes and is responsible for an MA (SEN) programme for Dutch teachers taught in the Netherlands. Previously she taught in primary, secondary and special schools and worked as an adviser for SEN. Research interests centre around all aspects of developing more effective learning and she is currently leader of a project looking at using Information and Communication Technology (ICT) to improve and enhance access to learning.

Stephanie Lorenz is a qualified and experienced educational psychologist who has worked in both LEA and Health Authority settings. She gained her PhD at the Hester Adrian Research Centre at Manchester University and has developed a special interest in inclusive education, particularly of children with Down's Syndrome. Since taking early retirement in 1994, she has worked as a freelance consultant as well as sitting on the Special Educational Needs Tribunal.

Hannah Mortimer is an educational psychologist in North Yorkshire. She specialises in working with children under 5 who have special educational needs, in both education and health settings. She writes regularly for early years magazines, and is extensively involved in training and practice-based research.

Mary Robinson has worked as a teacher in both mainstream and special schools. For the last 6 years she has worked as an educational psychologist in the London Borough of Newham where she leads a team of psychologists working with preschool children through the Child Development Centre. Her interest in the education of deaf children has developed through her work with two mainstream schools with inclusive provision for deaf children.

Zahirun (Runi) Sayeed is at present a senior educational psychologist with responsibility for continuing professional development in the London Borough of Tower Hamlets Educational Psychology Service. As an experienced teacher she has worked in the UK and abroad. In the 1980s she was involved in the development and management of a nationwide programme for children with special educational needs in Bangladesh. As an educational psychologist she has long been involved in under-fives work and Portage. Runi's journal publications include *Induction and Supervision for Newly Qualified EP's* and she regularly contributes to the postgraduate training of psychologists.

Sue Sheppard is an educational psychologist working for the London Borough of Redbridge. She also works for the National Autistic Society at their diagnostic, assessment, training and research centre, as well as being a course tutor for the Open University. She has a varied background in special education and has been involved over time in provision development and the evaluation of teaching approaches for pupils with autistic spectrum disorders.

Ann Warn is an educational psychologist who is currently working as the Early Years Assessment Manager in North West Kent.

Sheila Wolfendale has been a primary school and remedial reading teacher, an educational psychologist in several local education authorities and is currently director of a Doctorate in Educational Psychology programme in the Psychology Department at the University of East London. She has authored and edited many books, booklets, chapters, articles and handbooks on aspects of special needs, early years, educational psychology and parental involvement. She was awarded a professorship in 1988 and in 1995 gained a PhD by published works.

Janine Wooster is currently working as the Special Educational Services Manager in North West Kent, having previously co-ordinated the PreSchool Home Visiting Team in the London Borough of Newham.

Editor's Foreword

Since this book was first published in early 1997, there has been a change of Government. The Labour Government elected in May 1997 adopted a firm policy commitment to bringing about an integrated system of early years provision and child care, within which young children with special needs are to have an inclusive place, as of right. Further reference to the Government's strategy, within the context of this book, which is made throughout Chapter 1, has been accordingly updated, to take account of these and related developments. The other chapters in this book will be variously affected, over time, by government policy, but essentially the principles, strategies and provision described here stand as solid beacons of contemporary thinking and practice.

Sheila Wolfendale,
London,
April 2000

Chapter 1

The State and Status of Special Educational Needs in the Early Years

Sheila Wolfendale

Introducing the book

We welcome readers to a book that celebrates the burgeoning field of early years special educational needs practice, and we invite those of you who work in this area to read, relate to, identify with ideas and their applications; perhaps to be stimulated and challenged in your own practice. The book is aimed at those who work within early years/SEN, as teachers, their non-teaching colleagues, educational psychologists, administrators, policy-makers and practitioners in training.

The authors all have a strong teaching and SEN background; many of them now work or have worked as educational psychologists; others work as lecturers, administrators, advisers. Collectively they bring a wealth of experience in working with young children or on their behalf across a range of special needs and disabilities.

I would like to acknowledge at the outset the help and support given to the preparation of this book by members of a group of educational psychologists who have a brief or remit for working with early years/SEN within their local education authorities, and who meet, twice a year, at the University of East London to share, debate and discuss issues and developments in that area. The group endorsed the idea of and need for a book that would bring together contemporary practice, and indeed several of the authors are members of that group.

Reason and rationale for the book

Few texts currently exist in this area. There are several chapters in a number of edited early years or special needs books (Herbert and Moir, 1996; Wolfendale and Wooster, 1996) and two other recent texts on early years/SEN (Wilson, 1998; Roffey, 1999). There is a wealth of effective and innovative local practice that could and should be disseminated and shared more widely and which could provide the source and stimulus for other work. There is, correspondingly, considerable practitioner expertise and there is scope for practitioners to describe and discuss their work within a wider forum, such as this book.

Various pieces of legislation with associated Guidance are now in force, the policy and practice effects of which need to be explored within the public domain – the 1993 Education Act, Part Three; the 1994 Code of Practice and its section on Under Fives; due for revision during 2000 and implementation during 2001; the 1989 Children Act requirements for provision for (young) children in need; the OFSTED inspection and early years/SEN *Framework for Inspection*; the Qualifications and Curriculum Authority Early Learning Goals (QCA 1999) which has implications for curriculum for young children with special needs.

The state and status of SEN within the early years

Wolfendale and Wooster (1996) provided a chronological résumé of the increasing profile of SEN in the early years, and this provides the context for this section.

The Warnock Report (1978) gave under-fives and special needs a higher profile than previously by recommending it as a priority area in terms of teacher training and increased provision. Emphasis was given to the proven effectiveness of intervention programmes, including Portage, to partly justify this call for increased investment in the early years as both a preventive and 'remedial' measure.

Warnock paved the way for the legislation that amended existing law on special education, namely the 1981 Education Act (implemented from April 1983), which conferred new duties on local education and health authorities in respect of identifying and assessing young children with possible special needs. The accompanying circular to this act was updated in 1989 (Circular 22/89) to take account of the 1988 Education Reform Act as well as recent developments and contained a whole section on under-fives with special needs, reflecting developments that had taken place.

The next significant legislative landmark in the arena of special educational needs was the 1993 Education Act, Part Three of which referred exclusively to SEN (please note, the 1993 Education Act was subsumed along with other Education Acts, into the consolidated 1996 Education Act). That Part of the Act repealed the 1981 Education Act, retaining core principles and formal assessment procedures, but strengthening a number of parental rights and clarifying the processes. Schools are now required by law to have written accountable SEN policies. The 1994 Code of Practice constituted a set of guidelines to which LEAs and schools must have 'due regard' in the planning and delivery of SEN services, from pre-school onwards.

The Code of Practice acknowledges the importance of partnership between LEAs, child health and social services in working together to meet the needs of children under five with SEN. A whole section in the existing Code of Practice is devoted to 'Assessments and Statements for Under Fives'. The revised Code, mentioned above, will still have an early years section and indications are that this will be strengthened and cross referenced to existing early years initiatives such as *Sure Start* (Glass, 1999, and see below) and the QCA Early Learning Goals.

There is now plenty of evidence to show that at every level of practice, management and policy-making, special needs in the early years is in receipt of more attention, resources and provision than at any other time. Personnel working within these areas are bound to implement and have due regard to such legislation, including the 1989 Children Act and *its* emphasis upon: needs definition, service provision for young children 'in need' and with disabilities, registration and review. Strong encouragement is given in these various Acts of Parliament for practitioners to work together more effectively. Some local authorities began to consider and implement joint commissioning of early years, mental health and children's services, and indeed Children's Services Plans have been mandatory since April 1996.

The framework for such inter-agency and collective responsibility is now The Early Years Development and Childcare Partnership, required for each locality (DfEE, 1999) which, amongst other requirements, must provide for SEN in early years settings.

The Partnerships must, in written form, provide information about the following: details of the support which will be provided to ensure that all early years education providers have means and procedures to identify and address special educational needs; the range of childcare and early education provision available and appropriate for children with SEN and disabilities; how the Partnership plans to make provision more inclusive; training opportunities in SEN for early years staff; advice and written information available to parents/carers about child care and education opportunities for their children and support for themselves.

This is the broader context within which quality in the delivery of early years SEN services is to be judged, and some of the key themes relating to that context are further explored in this chapter.

There is considerable progress to celebrate; both the state and the status of SEN within the early years have been elevated in recent years. This book, whilst celebrating developments and innovations, also provides a reminder that these foundation years must be properly invested in and resourced.

Content and organisation of the book

The book's coverage is intended to portray some of the range and depth of contemporary early years/SEN work at all stages from identification, assessment, intervention, provision, review. It is an explicitly practice-focused text, showing, we hope, the complex interplay between theory, principles, policy and practice in an area which encompasses statutory procedures (i.e. statutory assessment under the 1993 Education Act) within non-statutory provision.

It was decided at the outset that the book should include a greater number of chapters, sacrificing chapter length for range and diversity. Collectively the chapters show differing angles and perspectives upon key activities referred to in the preceeding paragraph. The chapters have been loosely 'clumped' and progress somewhat schematically, throughout the book. We have tried to be as inclusive as possible and hope that readers will forgive us for any perceived omissions.

The next three chapters (2–4) provide accounts of facilities and provision and encompass assessment and intervention, illustrating models of practice (and see Sayeed and Guerin, 2000). Chapters 5–9 explore assessment and intervention with and provision for young children with identified areas of special needs and disabilities. Chapter 10 presents the relationship between policy and practice, and can be said to provide a macro-systemic perspective. Chapter 11 discusses implementing educational psychologist practice in assessment from a set of articulated principles and theoretical formulations. Chapters 12 and 13 focus on inter- and multi-agency working. Chapter 14 explores basic principles underpinning nursery education with reference to special needs and critically appraises the Nursery Voucher Scheme (this scheme is now defunct; the chapter stands as a useful historical marker). Chapter 15 provides a reminder of principles of an inclusive approach towards young children with special educational needs, which should underpin good quality provision. Several of the above themes will be commented upon in the remainder of this chapter.

Assessment

The Code of Practice constitutes the blueprint for effective early years SEN practice. It could be said to codify existing good assessment practice in the early years, into which context specifically assessing for special educational needs forms a legitimate part. In other words, assessment for special needs is *inclusive* assessment practice.

The range of approaches to assessment – direct observation of children at play or involved in specific learning tasks, systematic record-keeping, checklist completion, cognitive testing – are not the monopoly of SEN specialists (Hinton, 1993) and practitioners such as the chapter authors would not want to divorce their assessment approaches from such mainstream practice. What is specialised about assessing young children with a view to identifying their special needs is competence in:

- closely focusing on specific behaviours
- relating these to a child's overall functioning
- appraising functioning, within a broader, ecological or situation-specific context
- analysing and interpreting a range of assessment findings
- synthesising all the evidence
- presenting to and sharing the information with others
- taking single/collective action as a consequence of the assessment evidence.

Some of the chapters in this book show (a) how a number of 'acts of assessment' cohere in these ways, and that (b) assessment leads to action, (c) that the participants in *acts of assessment* share and act upon the information. Such interlocking assessment practice betokens a shift in the last few years, away from single-discipline assessment, the results of which might or might not be shared. The Code of Practice reinforces the view that assessment *per se* (of whatever sort, testing, observation, etc.) is sterile unless it is a collective activity.

The nursery/playgroup/day care practitioners play a significant 'front line' part in keeping close, detailed records on children which constitute the basis from which more 'specialist' assessment can take place – by special needs teachers, educational psychologists, speech therapists, and others. Principles of assessment, as set out by Drummond and Nutbrown (1996) and Wolfendale (1993) for example, inform *all* early years practice, including, integrally, special educational needs. What crucially drives these principles is something which might be called 'the ethics of assessment' (Nutbrown's equivalent phrase is 'respectful assessment', 1996) which emphasises that:

- The 'best interests' of children be paramount at all times.
- Children's prior experience and achievements be valued and celebrated.
- Diversity and difference in children's experience be welcomed and respected.

- All children are entitled to differential assessment as meets their learning and personal needs.
- Children have the right to have representation from and recourse to others, on their behalf on assessment issues.
- Assessment practice is an equitable, just reflection of a child's functioning.
- Assessment is effected in partnership ... and reciprocal exchange of information on the basis of equality is integral.
- The results of assessment be acted upon, openly and accountably.

(Wolfendale, 1993: 40)

Intervention

Intervention, as applied to early years/SEN, can be broadly conceived, and I have provided a definition that encompasses mainstream, specialist, home settings, involvement of various agencies and a range of curriculum approaches (and see Wolfendale, 2000). Several of the chapters in this book epitomise the range and diversity of 'intervention' which usually is seen to be post-assessment action and provision.

In this early years/SEN realm, intervention is purposeful and designed to effect as close a match as possible between a young child's identified *special* needs and that provision or resource which will meet his or her needs and best facilitate learning and development. In other words, the intervention should manifestly 'make a difference'.

Again, an inclusive approach is one that acknowledges a young child's right to differential treatment but within a context of 'provision for all' (see Chapters 14 and 15). Hannah Mortimer (1995) exemplifies such an inclusive philosophy in an article outlining ways in which mainstream nursery and reception staff can welcome and support special needs children. Barry Carpenter expresses this holistic view in these words:

'more than ever we need dynamic early intervention services that can enable families to work in an active dialogue with professionals towards meeting the needs of their children.'

(Carpenter, 1994: 10)

Intervention approaches for young children with special needs have also evolved in an increasingly sophisticated way as several chapters attest.

Indeed the 'message' that early intervention pays dividends has been comprehensively adopted by the current government, as evinced in the DfEE SEN Green Paper (1997) and the ensuing Programme of Action (1998). The Green Paper singled out the STAR Children's Centre, the subject of Chapter 3 of this book, as an example of good practice, and the Programme of Action referred to the Government's 'flagship' ambitious early years intervention programme, *Sure Start* alluded to earlier. This programme aims to put into practice a number of the hard won lessons gained from earlier intervention projects, most notably the American *Head Start* programme and it is part of the Government's plan to tackle childhood poverty, social exclusion, and ensure sound foundations for development and learning. These are some of the key features of the UK *Sure Start* programme:

* the aim is to have 250 *Sure Start* programmes running eventually (it is a ten year programme, started during 1999)
* at Government level, it is an inter-departmental initiative, with Education (DfEE) as the lead department
* inter-departmental partnership is expected to be a core feature of local *Sure Start* schemes
* *Sure Start* areas are ones identified as being areas of deprivation
* core services aim to offer parenting support, and encourage and support parents with their child-rearing responsibilities, including their early development and learning
* each programme has to make a clear statement on special needs and develop ways of working with families in partnership
* as with Early Years Development and Childcare Partnerships, information for parents/carers on provision, including special needs, must be readily available.

Thus, there is a prime emphasis in *Sure Start* on prevention as well as early action/intervention (see Glass 1999 for further information).

Collective responsibility for the delivery of early years special needs services

A key message emerging from this book is surely that of corporate responsibility. The chapters illustrate the interrelation between services at every level, whether this works effectively or not.

We are all committed to these foundation years. The Royal Society of Arts report (1994) on the importance of early learning, spelled out the nature of our commitment – it is educational, it is societal, it is an obligation to the adult citizens of tomorrow to give them the best possible start. The report also spelled out how commitment should be matched with material investment in high-quality early years provision.

Within a vision of such investment, the notion of shared, collective responsibility is integral. This vision is described in Hillary Clinton's book

It Takes a Village ... (1996). She redefines the old African proverb 'it takes a village to raise a child' in the context of our contemporary world, with instant mass communication and high degree of mobility, and says:

> the village can no longer be defined as a place on a map, or a list of people or organisations, but its essence remains the same – it is the network of values and relationships that support and affect our lives.

(Clinton, 1996: 12)

There have long been pious exhortations upon practitioners to collaborate in the planning and delivery of children's services. Yet, on the ground, co-operation and co-working have been hampered by lack of systemic, structural frameworks and by the divides created by having a range of disciplines, all representing the same area.

A number of models have been proposed to describe the varying degrees of professional closeness both extant and possible – see for example the Levels of Co-operation outlined in Lloyd (1994): no contact – communication – co-operation – annexation – co-ordination – merger. Lloyd's research identified characteristics of good practice for inter-agency work.

The advent of Early Years Development and Childcare Partnerships referred to above and operational in all localities, will, without doubt, effect the long-desired corporate responsibility for all young children.

The place of parents

Several chapters in this book indicate that parents occupy a central place in service delivery. There is intentionally no separate chapter on parents; one main reason is that a book on parents and special needs in the David Fulton Publishers' *Home and School – Working Alliance* series, was published around the same time as the first version of this book. That book (Wolfendale, 1997) is an edited collection of chapters written by parents and professionals and it reviews developments in partnership with parents, especially since the Code of Practice; it describes SEN parent partnership schemes and considers future directions in parent–professional relations. The DfEE Programme of Action already referred to sets out the expectation (to be ratified in law during 2000) that all LEAs will have to have a Parent Partnership Service in place, along with Conciliation services, to try to resolve a number of 'disputes' with parents before they reach the SEN Tribunal. Readers are also referred to Bastiani and Wolfendale (1996) and Wolfendale and Bastiani (2000) for general texts on parental involvement; and to Hornby (1994), Gascoigne (1995) and Dale (1996) for parental involvement in the area of special needs.

Notwithstanding this array of parallel texts, it is essential to make several points about the inclusion of parents, carers and families into the service delivery.

Collaborative approaches must surely include the home, as the earlier quote from Barry Carpenter stated. The Portage scheme epitomises the 'different but equal' contribution of parents as partners in this early years home-based intervention in which parents are the educators of their own children and also co-planners of the service as a whole. (For a detailed review of Portage see Wolfendale, 1997:10-26).

The principles of partnership as elaborated in the Code of Practice are intended to apply to all parents/carers of children with SEN, right across the age span. Likewise, irrespective of age of children, parents have intermittent if not enduring needs to have access to support for a wide-ranging array of parenting tasks, responsibilities and child behaviours. Recent surveys Family Policies Studies Centre, 1996) confirm the needs of families for access to such support (and see Smith's survey, 1996, of over fifty parent training and support programmes).

Caesar (1993:18) lists four principles that she says should underpin work with children and their families, especially in the early years. These are:

- *Universalism:* We all use and need services, and families of children 'in need' have full rights to the wide range and diversity of universalist provisions, as well as to specialist services.
- *Equality and equity of access to services:* Everyone in our community has rights to accessible family support services; parents requesting help should not be stigmatised and their access to services must be facilitated.
- *The normality of difficulties in parenting:* Services should support and supplement families' endeavours, especially when parenting difficulties are compounded by poverty and deprivation.
- *Participation*: Parents usually know what their needs are and their views should be taken seriously.

Assuring quality in early years SEN services

Agreeing principles and values is one of the fundamental first steps in setting out a number of quality assurance indicators (Elfer and Wedge, 1996). Such indicators or *characteristics* determining the *quality* of services on offer have been identified in a number of reports and publications – see Moss and Pence (1994) for inclusion of *equality*, and Williams (1995) for an overview of ten approaches to the definition and measurement of quality in early years provision. Katz (1994) proposed multiple perspectives on the quality of early years provision. These are:

1. The view from above (e.g. supervisors, inspectors).
2. The view from below (experienced by the children).
3. The view from inside (experienced by the staff).
4. The view from outside-in (experienced by parents).
5. The outside (society and posterity).

These approaches to 'quality audit' surely equally apply to special needs contexts, especially within an *inclusive* ideology. The same determinants of 'value added' (DfE, 1995) as apply to early years services must be applicable to SEN-oriented services. Indeed the Audit Commission (1996) defines special needs broadly and perceives that the SEN 'population' is part of such universal pre-school services.

These overarching quality assurance mechanisms can provide the broader framework within which we can identify special needs-specific criteria of effective practice. Mittler and Mittler (1994: 24–25) list 21 Good Practice Indicators – also see Daly in the same volume discussing quality in relation to Portage services, Mollie White's chapter in Wolfendale (1997), and Wolfendale and Wooster (1996) for a suggested list of values and principles which could form the basis of a 'partnership charter' and which could, in turn, be used as indicators of quality.

OFSTED is to rationalise the several early years inspection systems currently in operation, with effect from 2001, into an unified separate arm of OFSTED.

An entitlement for children in the early years: towards an inclusive social policy

Further evidence that the early years and special needs realm has attained respectable status and is now seen as an area in its own right comes from the policy statement on *Early Years* developed by NASEN (National Association for Special Educational Needs) during 1999 (NASEN 1999). It sets out key principles and outlines the various responsibilities of government and local agencies in ensuring realisation of policy in practice. Inclusion is the broadest, unifying principle.

Threading through this chapter and the book are key concepts associated with *equal opportunities* and children's *rights* to have full access to educational opportunities. Shah (1995), with reference to service delivery, and Siraj-Blatchford (1994) with reference to early years provision, graphically illustrate how such rhetoric has to be translated into practice and what vigilance and resources are required to be *inclusive* on behalf of all children in their foundation years.

The Government has also affirmed a commitment to inclusive education, one of the themes of this book (and see Dickins and Denizloe 1998). We are seeing the evolution of a coherent, integrated child care and early years education policy, which embraces 'provision for all' and which surely can only benefit all young children in their crucial foundation years.

References

Audit Commission (1996) *Counting to Five, Education of Children under 5.* London: HMSO.

Bastiani, J. and Wolfendale, S. (eds) (1996) *Home–School Work in Britain, Review, Reflection and Development.* London: David Fulton Publishers.

Caesar, G. (1993) *Early Childhood Provision in Britain in the 1990s.* London: National Children's Bureau.

Carpenter, B. (ed.) (1994) *Early Intervention, Where are We Now?* Oxford: Westminster College.

Clinton, H. (1996) *It Takes a Village ... and Other Lessons Children Teach Us.* London: Simon and Schuster.

Dale, N. (1996) *Working with Families of Children with Special Needs.* London: Routledge.

Daly, B. (1994) 'Portage and Home Visiting'. In Mittler, P. and Mittler, H. (eds) *Innovations in Family Support for People with Learning Disabilities.* Chorley: Lisieux Publications.

DfE (1994) *Code of Practice on the Identification and Assessment of Special Educational Needs.* London: HMSO.

DfE (1995) *Value Added in Education.* London: Department for Education and Employment.

DfEE (1997) *Excellence for All Children, Meeting SEN.* London: The Stationery Office, October.

DfEE (1998) *Meeting SEN, A Programme of Action*, DfEE Publications.

DfEE (1999) *Early Years Development and Childcare Partnership: Planning Guidance, 1999–2000*, DfEE Publications.

Dickins, M. and Denziloe, J. (1998) *All Together – how to create inclusive services for disabled children and their families, a practical handbook for early years workers.* London: National Early Years Network, 77 Holloway Road, London N7 8JZ.

Drummond, M. and Nutbrown, C. (1996) 'Observing and assessing young children'. In Pugh, G. (ed.) *Contemporary Issues in the Early Years*, 2nd edn. London: Paul Chapman.

Elfer, P. and Wedge, D. (1996) 'Defining, Measuring and Supporting Quality'. In Pugh, G. (ed.) *Contemporary Issues in the Early Years*, 2nd edn. London: Paul Chapman.

Family Policy Studies Centre (1996) *Parenting Problems, a National Study of Parents and Parenting Problems.* London: FPSC, 231 Baker Street, London, NW1 6XE.

Gascoigne, E. (1995) *Working with Parents as Partners in SEN.* London: David Fulton Publishers.

Glass, N. (1999) SURE START: the development of an early intervention programme for young children in the UK, *Children and Society*, Vol. 13, No. 4, September, pp 257–265.

Herbert, E. and Moir, J. (1996) 'Children with SEN – a collaborative and inclusive style of working'. In Nutbrown, C. (ed.) *Children's Rights and Early Education*. London: Paul Chapman.

Hinton, S. (1993) 'Assessing for Special Needs and supporting learning in the early years and nursery education'. In Wolfendale, S. (ed.) *Assessing Special Educational Needs*. London: Cassell.

Hornby, G. (1994) *Working with Parents of Children with Special Educational Needs*. London: Cassell.

Katz, L. (1994) 'Assessing the Development of Preschoolers'. *ERIC Digest*, October, University of Illinois (4 page digest)

Lloyd, C. (1994) *The Welfare Network: How Well Does the Net Work?* Oxford: School of Education, Oxford Brookes University.

Mittler, P. and Mittler, H. (eds) (1994) *Innovations in Family Support for People with Learning Disabilities*. Chorley: Lisieux Publications.

Mortimer, H. (1995) 'Welcoming young children with special needs into mainstream education'. *Support for Learning*, **10**(4), 164–169.

NASEN (1999) *Policy Document on Early Years*. Tamworth: NASEN.

Nutbrown, C. (ed.) (1996) *Children's Rights and Early Education*. London: Paul Chapman.

OFSTED (1995) *Framework for Inspection*. London; HMSO.

OFSTED (1996) *The Implementation of the Code of Practice for Children with Special Educational Needs*. London: HMSO.

QCA (1999) *Early Learning Goals*. London: QCA.

Roffey, S. (1999) *Special Needs in the Early Years: Collaboration, communication and coordination*. London: David Fulton Publishers.

Royal Society of Arts (1994) *Start Right, The Importance of Early Learning*. London: Royal Society of Arts.

Sayeed, Z. and Guerin, E. (2000) *Early Years Play, a happy medium for assessment and intervention*. London: David Fulton Publishers.

Siraj-Blatchford, I. (1994) *The Early Years: Laying Foundations for Racial Equality*. Stoke-on-Trent: Trentham Books.

Shah, R. (1995) *The Silent Minority, Children with Disabilities in Asian Families*. London: National Children's Bureau.

Smith, C. (1996) *Developing Parenting Programmes*. London: National Children's Bureau.

Warnock, M. (Chair) (1978) *Special Educational Needs*. London: HMSO.

White, M. (1997) 'A Review of the Influence and Effects of Portage'. In Wolfendale, S. (ed.) *Working with Parents of SEN Children after the Code of Practice*. London: David Fulton Publishers.

Williams, P. (1995) *Making Sense of Quality, A Review of Approaches to Quality in Early Childhood Services*. London: National Children's Bureau.

Wilson, R. (1998) *Special Educational Needs in the Early Years*. London: Routledge.

Wolfendale, S. (ed.) (1993a) *Assessing Special Educational Needs*. London: Cassell.

Wolfendale, S. (1993b) *Baseline Assessment, A Review of Current Practice, Issues and Strategies for Effective Implementation*. Stoke on Trent: Trentham Books.

Wolfendale, S and Wooster, J (1996) 'Meeting special needs in the early years'. In Pugh, G. (ed.) *Contemporary Issues in the Early Years*, 2nd edn. London: Paul Chapman.

Wolfendale, S. (ed.) (1997) *Working with Parents of SEN Children after the Code of Practice*. London: David Fulton Publishers.

Wolfendale, S. (Ed) (2000) *Special Needs in the Early Years – Snapshots of practice*. London: Routledge.

Wolfendale, S. and Bastiani, J. (Eds) (2000) *The Parental Contribution to School Effectiveness*. London: David Fulton Publishers.

Chapter 2

A Pre-school Assessment Model

Moira Challen

This chapter describes a pre-school assessment model developed by the London Borough of Barking and Dagenham in response to the 1981 Education Act. The model, in operation for over 10 years, has been successful in providing high-quality assessment and intervention over time, facilitating multiprofessional and parental involvement and providing quality advice towards pre-school statutory assessments. The chapter also touches on more recent developments in pre-school assessment with Social Services day nurseries in response to The Children Act 1989. The chapter concludes by considering reasons for success, benefits of the model and future initiatives.

Introduction

The London Borough of Barking and Dagenham is a small London borough 9 miles east of central London, on the northern bank of the River Thames. It has a population of approximately 35,000 in the 0–19 age range. Pre-school provision has always assumed a high priority in the borough and the Local Education Authority(LEA) is committed to high-quality nursery education for all. The borough is currently served by nurseries attached to all infant and primary schools and all but two of its voluntary aided primary schools. Children can be admitted part-time to nursery classes in the September prior to their fourth birthday.

Pre-school children with special needs are supported by a range of educational services in the borough including a Portage service, Hearing and Visual Impairment Services and three specialist Nursery Assessment Bases (two integrated, one special). Barking and Dagenham is committed to supporting integrated provision and working in partnership with parents. Increasing numbers of pre-school children with special educational needs are attending mainstream nurseries.

Barking and Dagenham also provides four day nurseries and one children and family centre which offer full- and part-time care. Children who have a disability or a particular need for day care are given priority consideration.

In addition all borough provision is supported by the Health services including Speech and Language Therapists, Physiotherapists and other professionals.

Background

The 1981 Education Act had a major influence on the assessment of pre-school children in Barking and Dagenham. To comply fully and seriously with the identification and assessment of the special educational needs of pre-school children as stated in the Act, two SEN nursery bases and an additional nursery teacher at a special school were proposed and agreed to. The new Nursery Assessment Bases (NABs) were operational from September 1984, with admissions procedures, model of assessment and other professionals' roles initially established. The Model of Assessment developed by the NABs and described in this chapter established a pattern of good practice in pre-school assessment and has since helped to inform assessment practice within other settings.

The provision comprises two integrated bases and one special school nursery base. The integrated provision is fully operational within mainstream nurseries. Each base can cater for up to 16 pupils with a maximum of eight attending each a.m. or p.m. session. Each base has a Teacher-in-Charge, a Nursery Nurse and Special Support Assistance.

The process prior to assessment

The 1981 Education Act (Section 10) stated that Local Health Authorities had a duty to inform parents and notify LEAs of a child over the age of 2 who may have SENs and the LEA had a duty to act upon this. The 1993 Education Act reiterates these duties and provides detailed guidance to Health Authorities, LEAs, pre-school provisions and others about their responsibilities.

In Barking and Dagenham, young children are monitored by the Health Authority and referred to a number of services prior to notification, including the Portage Service, Hearing and Visually Impaired Services, Physiotherapy, Speech Therapy, etc. Young children's progress is also reviewed at 6-monthly intervals at Multidisciplinary Review Meetings attended by personnel from health, education and social services. The decision to notify a child to the LEA may be taken at these meetings and is instigated by a Senior Clinical Medical Officer or is taken outside the meeting instigated then by a speech therapist or community consultant paediatrician.

Following notification, the LEA writes to the parents to inform them of the next steps. An Educational Psychologist (EP) is asked to contact the family and arrange to carry out an initial assessment of the child's progress and needs to establish whether there is a prima-facie case for statutory assessment. An EP's initial assessment includes a home visit involving discussion with parents, observation and activities with the young child. This initial process is guided by a Barking and Dagenham Pre-School Assessment Schedule which focuses on collecting a developmental history and information about the child's current skills and areas of concern collaboratively with the family.

The Assessment Schedule was designed, incorporating current psychological trends, to address the specific needs of the EPs in their approach to pre-school assessment. It provides a structure for collating information through discussion and observation in the following areas based on a developmental perspective:

* Background information
* Self-help
* Physical
* Social behaviour
* Communication
* Play and early learning
* Next steps
* Agreed action

also forming the basis of the EP report. The importance of parental involvement in pre-school assessment is now recognised and the schedule facilitates partnership through its clear layout and provision of section summary boxes for joint completion. The assessment schedule also contains guidelines for assessing children with sensory impairment (see Farrelly, 1993).

Further information is collected through discussion with other professionals, observation of the child in other familiar/natural settings (e.g. playgroup) and direct work with the child on selected activities to supplement information already obtained. A profile of the child's development is drawn together and future educational arrangements are discussed with the family. The information is drawn together in an EP report and is distributed to parents, relevant professionals and the LEA, with recommendations to the LEA as to whether Statutory Assessment is required.

Possible recommendations following notification include:

- No further action required.
- Longer EP assessment period required.
- Monitoring arrangements required at playgroup, nursery or school.
- Active involvement of EP at nursery/school at Stage 3 of the Code of Practice.
- Statutory assessment recommended.

Prior to the Children Act 1989 and the 1993 Education Act the majority of pre-school children were placed for statutory assessment in the borough's nursery assessment bases. The two integrated nursery bases catered for children with general developmental delay (including speech and language) and the special school nursery base catered for children with more profound and multiple developmental delay. Children were placed according to these criteria, and according to where they lived in the borough for placement in one of the integrated bases. Children could be placed for assessment throughout the year after their third birthday and on availability of places (this is still the case in the bases).

In more recent years, changing attitudes within the LEA, increased attention to parental views, and external influences such as The Children Act and the Code of Practice have led to a greater flexibility in placement for statutory assessment. Statutory assessment of pre-school children in Barking and Dagenham may now take place in a range of provision including:

- Nursery assessment bases.
- Local educational nurseries.
- Social Services day nurseries.
- Other provision.
- Home (in exceptional circumstances).

However, the model of assessment that has been developed in the bases has helped to inform statutory assessment practice in other settings.

A description of the NAB model of assessment

Following agreement for placement in a nursery assessment base (NAB), a three-stage model of joint assessment takes place, culminating in joint educational and psychological advice. The assessment includes a planning meeting, a review meeting and a report-writing meeting.

These meetings are multiprofessional and involve parents fully. They aim to review progress, establish current skills and set targets. The targets form the basis for an individual education plan (IEP). They take into account progress and skills both at home and in the nursery and also take on board skills that can be worked on jointly at home and in nursery (e.g. toilet training etc.).

When the model was initially set up (i.e. prior 1993 Education Act) the process aimed to take place over a period of up to 8 months encompassing a philosophy of assessment over time (for example, Figure 2.1).

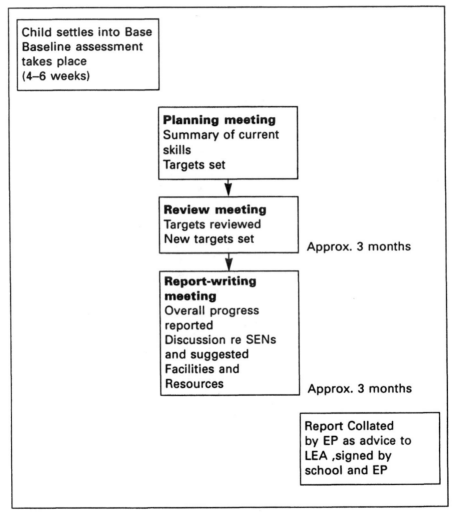

Figure 2.1 Nursery assessment base – assessment process

With the implementation of the Code of Practice, however, timings and meetings have had to be streamlined in accordance, to allow the LEA to complete the full statutory assessment process to issue of the Statement of Special Educational Needs within 6 months. In many cases this has meant that the timing or format of the review meeting has had to be more flexible, or the formal Statutory Assessment process is initiated at a later date following the planning meeting, with the understanding that children are placed for assessment with statutory assessment taking place during the child's period in the base. The overall aim however is for the whole process to be completed prior to a child becoming of statutory school age and preferably in time for reception entry in September alongside other pupils.

The process

As soon as a child is placed in a NAB, a base line assessment of their current skills is carried out. A curriculum document (currently being revised with a view to establishing a wider use within the authority) was developed by the NAB staff to aid their assessment and intervention.

The purpose of the curriculum document is to provide a baseline assessment of a child's current skills, a guideline for next steps (i.e. how to help the child progress), an ongoing record of achievement, information for others, including parents and an aid for the final report writing. It acts as both a formative and summative record. The curriculum document is a thorough checklist which covers a range of skills which can be broadly categorised into:

- Early attention skills
- Physical skills
- Self-help and independence skills
- Communication skills
- Social/behaviour skills
- Play and early learning skills

The baseline assessment forms the basis for the Planning meeting which is attended by parents, school staff and EP. Other relevant professionals, as appropriate, are invited (Portage, speech, therapist, physiotherapist etc.). There are guidelines (see Appendix 1, at the end of this chapter) which clearly set out the format for the meeting. The school prepares a report for discussion which summarises the child's current skills within the above areas and suggested teaching targets. Following discussion and agreement, the EP collates the information together with any amendments, a background summary to placement and agreements for further action. The report is distributed and the targets form the basis for the child's Individual Education Plan.

The review meeting is a more informal meeting held between the school and parents, the purpose being to review and revise targets. In some cases now, because of time pressures the review meeting is held more informally and combined with a home visit.

The Report-writing meeting is the final meeting (see Appendix 2). The purpose is to evaluate and summarise the child's progress over the period of assessment and intervention and to consider jointly the child's special educational needs and suggested facilities and resources. As the child will be continuing to attend nursery until completion of the statement, current targets are also discussed and agreed as part of the meeting. All those who attended the planning meeting are invited to contribute to discussion at this meeting. The school prepares a report as a basis for discussion and the EP minutes and subsequently collates all the information (including background information) into a formal report to be distributed as advice towards statutory assessment as joint educational and psychological advice. (Health professionals submit independent advice.)

The process in practice

All three NABs operate in line with the model, but function within differing nursery approaches. The two integrated NABs are considered a part of their mainstream nursery with staff sharing responsibilities for all children throughout a nursery session within a carefully planned structure, but with NAB staff taking the responsibility for the individual programmes and assessment of the base children.

For example in one nursery run along Highscope lines (Hohman, Banet and Weikart, 1995), the NAB teacher and NNEB both have overall responsibility for a group of children's planning and reviewing. Base children will form a part of these and the other groups in the nursery. The Base staff are also timetabled into the structure of the whole session which includes time for individual work with base children. All staff are involved in planning for the nursery.

The NAB within the special school forms a part of the school's nursery, which may also take children from a neighbouring borough and children whose assessment is complete. All children within this nursery have carefully planned IEPs and the model of assessment, therefore, fits neatly into the structure and operation of the nursery.

The multiprofessional approach

While a child is being assessed in a NAB, a number of other professionals are fully involved, depending on the needs of the child.

Educational psychologists are involved from before the assessment to completion and transfer to full-time education. Their role is to advise and co-ordinate the process, collating information into the final report.

Many children have received Portage. When a child starts nursery

Portage visits continue but on a fortnightly basis and the Portage visitor is involved in the assessment meetings where targets are discussed and agreed.

Advice is also sought from the hearing and visually impaired services, although children with more significant hearing or visual difficulties may attend alternative nurseries (e.g. at the school with a hearing impaired base or specialist school for visually impaired children) where there is ready access to necessary equipment and modifications. However, the model of assessment described above is still followed through with these children.

The local health trust offers considerable support to the NABs. A Speech and Language Therapist is attached to all three bases and offers the equivalent of half a day per week direct support to each base. The therapist is involved in the joint planning for the children, assessing, advising and working directly on speech, language and communication targets. Physiotherapists work in the same way, becoming involved in planning, assessing and working with the children; their allocation of time, however, is needs driven.

Other professionals who may be involved in the joint planning and working have included health visitors, occupational therapists and social services.

Liaison with receiving school staff takes place on completion of the statement and is the final stage of the process before a child leaves the base. This will involve visits from and to the receiving school and with planned integration if required.

Working in partnership with parents

Parents are fully involved in the process, from notification until the outcome of the statutory assessment and the issue of a Statement of Special Educational Needs.

The local health trust has initial responsibility for discussing notification with a family. Subsequent to this the LEA provide the family with detailed and relevant information at every stage of the process, seeking their views at appropriate times. The initial assessment by an EP involves joint discussions and decisions with the parents about the child's progress, future needs and recommendations for placement.

Following the decision for a child to attend a NAB for assessment the nurseries take up the contact through pre-admission visits and arrangements for attendance and liaison. Parents are fully involved in supporting their child's progress throughout the nursery placement. Besides attendance at the meetings where joint planning can take place, parents are invited to open afternoons along with other professionals, they receive home visits and regular contact is maintained through home school diaries and phone calls. In some instances joint home visits may be made with other professionals (Portage, speech therapist, EP etc.).

EPs also maintain regular contact with parents throughout the assessment period, and it is hoped that through collective liaison and consultation with the family the eventual outcome of the assessment supports the views of all involved.

Professional development

A steering group meets on a termly basis (made up of Headteachers, NAB staff, EP and LEA representatives; annually, this includes other professionals) to discuss a range of issues including the day-to-day running and management of the bases, LEA procedures, the development of practice and the professional development of staff.

Areas for further development are agreed at the termly meetings. Recently these have included analysis of the effective use of support assistants, management of challenging behaviours and revision of the Curriculum Document. On a termly basis, specialist INSET is arranged for the nursery staff (including mainstream staff) and others. Topics have recently included autism and specialist teaching approaches, assessing and working with children with speech, language and communication difficulties.

A working party has been set up to review and revise the curriculum document. As a result of the 1993 Education Act and the Code of Practice a working party has also been set up to review and revise the NAB guidelines, procedures and admissions criteria to ensure that procedures adhere to legal and government guidelines at the same time as protecting the philosophy and efficient running of the bases. Issues that are being addressed include admissions criteria and parental choice of provision, timing of admission, reviews and assessment.

New developments

More recently, with changing attitudes within the LEA, increased parental preference and external influences such as The Children Act, flexibility in placement for statutory assessment has developed. Young children attend a range of pre-school provision, sometimes from a very young age and in some cases it is not always appropriate to move a child to a NAB for assessment. Increasing numbers of children with special needs attend their local nursery for assessment.

The Children Act 1989 placed a statutory duty on local authorities to provide for children in need, including children with disabilities. Locally, within the last few years, there has been an increase in the numbers of children with a range of disabilities attending Social Services Day Nurseries (SSDNs). Many of these children also receive educational support through the Portage service and structures for working together have been developed. As a result, the number of children being notified who attend SSDNs has increased and EPs' input into the SSDNs has developed. This has led to an examination of the working practice between education and day nursery professionals, culminating in a number of joint initiatives, including developing the NAB model of assessment for those children where it has been agreed that their assessment takes place at day nursery.

Pre-school model of assessment in Social Services day nurseries

EPs become involved with children attending day nurseries usually following notification, or a referral from the day nursery or parent. Where it has been agreed that a statutory assessment could take place at day nursery, the Portage service has been asked to provide the educational advice, including advice for children not known to the service. Initially there were no clear procedures for how the assessment would be carried out, or the nature of different professionals' involvement. As a result, a series of meetings were held involving the senior EP, the senior Portage worker, the principal officer for children in day care and the officers-in-charge of the day nurseries to establish a set of 'Guidelines' based on the NAB model of assessment but which aimed to clarify procedures and roles (see Appendix 3). Establishing the role of the Portage service in guiding the educational assessment and programme was particularly crucial to a successful and collaborative process, in that the day nursery staff would have the day-to-day management and evaluation of the programme although the process would be education led.

The model of assessment has been in operation in SSDNs for 1 year and a review of practice with Social Services personnel suggested that they find the process both constructive and supportive. Of particular value is the planning meeting where the procedure is explained fully, targets are set and subsequent professional input (including Portage) is discussed and agreed. The main issue which has arisen is one of additional resourcing to support the assessment of children with complex needs in day nursery. In some instances the day nursery see it as their responsibility under the

Children Act but it is felt by some that it should be an educational or joint responsibility. This is currently in discussion between Education and Social Services departments. Day nursery provision do not currently benefit from speech therapy input and similarly, representatives from education and health are exploring the extent of speech therapy need across the authority. Training for day nursery staff as staff groups has been an ongoing issue, which has to some extent been resolved with the recent introduction of a rota of 6-weekly training mornings amongst the day nurseries. This has already resulted in requests to the Educational Psychology Service for training on statutory assessment, Special Educational Needs and behaviour management.

Concluding remarks

Good quality multiprofessional assessment of pre-school children with special needs is an essential right for children and families if they are to gain future access to appropriate support, equipment and teaching. In an authority that supports an integrative approach, early assessment is crucial to the planning and preparation for a child's successful transition into full-time education.

The model of working described in this chapter strives to achieve the above and adhere to the principles embraced in the Education Act 1981, the Education Reform Act 1988, the Children Act 1989 and the Education Act 1993 in terms of early identification, assessing and meeting the special needs of children, involving parents in discussion and decision-making and working collaboratively with other agencies. By providing a co-ordinated approach across a range of provision it also becomes possible to meet the varied needs of individual families without detriment to their children.

The strength of the model lies in its clearly defined framework and procedures which form a part of a cohesive LEA special needs policy structure therefore facilitating effective transference to a range of settings. The benefits to staff and provision are being observed through closer working relationships and dialogue, joint training and development initiatives, sharing of skills and expertise, creating a philosophy and culture of reciprocal community access to resources and knowledge. The benefits to the LEA lie in the thorough and detailed nature of the assessment and the consistency of approach across different provision.

The practice of joint-reporting between psychologists and teachers has been an issue for debate. The collaborative approach is its strength, though it could be argued that it weakens the distinctive nature of an educational or psychological perspective.

The introduction of a revised NAB curriculum document as an LEA early years assessment guide for children undergoing statutory assessment is currently being explored. There will also need to be initiatives in the future arising from the increasing numbers of children with more complex needs attending all integrated provision. In particular a strong professional development programme is required with joint local authority training in specialist approaches across the range of ages and provision.

Appendix 1: Nursery assessment bases guidance for pre-school planning meetings

Preparation for meeting

Following initial assessment by the EP, recommendation for NAB and placement at base, the EP may wish to gain further information or review child's progress prior to the planning meeting.

Process of meeting

Introduction by Chair (EP or school chair meeting through prior agreement with school)

- Introduction of those present.
- Statement of the general background of the child's case in terms of what led to placement and relevant medical information, the various professionals involved with the child and their frequencies and nature of contact.
- Outline of the assessment process as a whole.
- Objectives of planning meeting.

EP or teacher reads through report

Time to be taken to reflect on each section of report in terms of:
- Clarification of information.
- Any new skills/information to be included since written comments prepared.
- Parental comments on skills at home.

EP or teacher reads through teaching targets set

Considering:
- Parents' comments.
- Any other targets required.

Any other issues and summary

Note any other issues and summarise main points.

Further action
- Record any further action that needs to be taken and by whom.
- Clarify arrangements for review meeting.
- Set date of report writing meeting.

Following meeting

EP collates any new information attaches schools report and distributes to:
- Family.
- School.
- CEO – Special Educational Needs Team.
- Any other relevant professionals.

Appendix 2: Nursery assessment bases guidance for final report writing meetings

Preparation for meeting

- EP collects up-to-date information on child's progress (this may include observation, discussion with Nursery/parents etc.).
- Base teacher prepares draft report comprising progress in each developmental area with accompanying teaching targets (at the end of each skill area) and a section on school and home factors.
- Both EP and base staff consider areas of Special Educational Need to contribute to discussion in meeting.
- Base staff prepare draft SENs and facilities and resources section for discussion at meeting. This may take place in consultation with the EP.

Process of meeting

- EP/school chairs meeting (to be negotiated)
- Chair explains purpose of report-writing meeting and subsequent process up until drawing up of statement.
- EP reviews background to referral and placement in nursery school.
- School or EP read through report and any comments or alterations are noted by the EP.
- *Special Educational Needs* – Chair facilitates discussion to consider written comments by the school. Special Educational Needs of the child are agreed and minuted by the EP.
- *Recommended facilities and resources* – Chair facilitates discussion to consider written comments regarding appropriate facilities and resources required to meet agreed special educational needs. EP to minute.
- Any other comments/general discussion.

Following meeting

- EP collates information into a draft report. comprising of following sections:
  I. Background
  II. Developmental progress
  III. Home/school factors
  IV. Special Educational Needs
  V. Recommended facilities and resources
- Draft report distributed to parents for comments and bases for signature.
- Report distributed to:
  Family
  School
  CEO – Special Educational Needs Team
  Local Health Trust
  Social services
  Any other professionals

Appendix 3: Guidelines for statutory assessment (1993 Education Act) taking place in Social Services day nurseries

Process

- A joint process to be adopted following the nursery assessment base model involving a:
  – Planning meeting
  – Review meeting
  – Report-writing meeting.
- The assessment will jointly involve:
  – Parents
  – Nursery staff (key worker and officer in charge)
  – Portage (education input)
  – Educational psychologist (EP)
- Other relevant professionals could be invited to attend meetings (e.g. physiotherapist, social worker etc.).
- The EP is responsible for co-ordinating all meetings (i.e. inviting, chairing, minuting and collecting information at meetings).

The planning meeting

- Prior to the meeting Portage (P) prepares report on child's progress in discussion with Key Worker (KW) following a minimum of:
  – One meeting between P and KW
  – One observation of child by P

- One meeting with parent by P.
- EP chairs the meeting which will involve:
  - Introductions
  - Explanation of the statutory assessment process
  - Background information regarding the referral and child
  - Report on child's progress (pre-prepared report)
  - Target setting
  - Agreed further action
  - Date for review and report-writing meeting.
- Subsequent Portage involvement agreed at meeting and minuted under further action. There should be fortnightly involvement/input. This could be a mix of:
  - Nursery Visit (Minimum monthly visits)
  - Home Visiting
  depending on needs of child.
- Any involvement of other professionals agreed at the meeting and minuted under further action.

The review meeting

- The purpose of this meeting is to review progress on targets and set new targets.
- EP chairs and minutes meeting.

The report-writing meeting

- The purpose of this meeting is to jointly draw together a report which will be forwarded to the LEA as joint advice from:
  - Education (Portage)
  - Social Services day nursery
  - EP service
- EP chairs and minutes the meeting which will involve discussion about:
  - Introduction and background information (prepared by EP)
  - Report on child's progress (pre-prepared by Portage and Day Nursery)
  - Special Educational Needs, suggested facilities and resources (draft prepared by EP for discussion).

Subsequent to the meeting

- EP will collate all the information discussed into a joint draft report to be distributed and signed by contributors (Portage, day nursery, EPS).
- EP will submit report to LEA as joint advice towards the statutory assessment.

References

Department of Education and Science (1981) *Education Act.* London: HMSO.

Department of Education and Science (1988) *Education Reform Act.* London: HMSO.

Department for Education (1993) *Education Act.* London: HMSO.

Department of Health (1989) *The Children Act.* London: HMSO.

Farrelly, D. (1993) *The Development of a New Pre-School Psychological Assessment Schedule.* Unpublished MSc Dissertation, University of East London.

Hohman, M., Banet, B. and Weikart, D. (1995) *Educating Young Children.* Ypsilante, Michigan: Highscope Press.

Chapter 3

STAR Children's Centre – Comprehensive Working with Young Children with Special Needs

Cathy Hamer

STAR (St Helens Advice and Resource) Children's Centre provides a comprehensive, inter-disciplinary service to pre-school children with special needs and disabilities and their families. Following an outline of the history of the Centre, the unique features of the building, management and staffing are described. The integrated approach is shown in the Journey Through the Stars which is illustrated in Figure 3.1.

A new star on the horizon

On 8 August 1899 an 'Infant Milk Depot' was opened in St Helens. It supplied sterilised humanised milk at 2d a day to needy children and functioned as a Clinic where children were weighed weekly. The first in the country, it was modelled on similar schemes in Normandy, France. The same year the Female Sanitary Inspectors began visiting all new-born babies to advise on infant feeding – the forerunners of Health Visitors!

It was to these auspicious beginnings that Child Heath Specialists looked in the1980s in seeking a name for a new venture bringing together professionals working with young children with disabilities. Paying tribute to the far-sighted Medical Officer of Health in 1899, the hospital-based centre became the Drew Harris Paediatric Assessment Unit. Opened in 1981, the centre was based on the recommendations of the Court Report (1976) that each health district, with the support of local education and social service authorities, should organise formally a multi-disciplinary team for all handicapped children. It was recommended that these 'district handicap teams' should have integrated facilities for prevention and treatment as well as assessment. In the unit, facilities were provided for children to be assessed by a multi-disciplinary team as well as attending for activity-based therapy sessions co-ordinated by a Nursing Sister. Transport was provided by ambulances and, following a case conference attended only by professionals, the findings were discussed with the parents by the consultant paediatrician.

Recognising the constraints of hospital-based provision, an overt medical emphasis, and with increasing awareness of the need for educational input, negotiations between the Health Authority and the Education Department resulted in a joint enterprise. In 1989 Windlebrook Child Development Centre opened in a mainstream primary school annexe with the addition of a nursery group, teacher and Portage service.

While the services developed, the building presented insurmountable difficulties, being poorly located, cramped and inflexible. A golden opportunity was presented in 1993 when a previous day nursery building was vacated. Purpose-built and designed for young children, it was available for immediate occupation. A single site, centrally located, one-stop community based multi-disciplinary service became a reality with the opening of STAR Children's Centre.

Building

This is Council owned and running costs are shared with the Health Authority. A survey of user and professionals' requirements conducted prior to the move revealed a request for a parents' room, informally furnished and homely rather than clinical, to be provided by themselves.

While accepting the need for specific requirements for professionals to operate successfully, the overriding objective was to provide a flexible and responsive service to young children and their families. A general consensus was achieved that change was necessary and that 'The way we do it now' was not the only way. A system of colour-coded and flexible-use rooms was designed with the only exceptions being the kitchen, administration office, staff-room and toilets. Activity and discovery areas were designated in the single central corridor and all other rooms were painted with a single colour – the door being a full gloss and the interior walls a lighter emulsion. The fun colours of red, pink, yellow and orange were to be used for children. Blue was allocated as a family room, green and purple were consultation rooms with the white room being a sensory stimulation room. The brown room became a staff work base with therapy, nursing, education, social work staff and students working alongside each other in close proximity. The grey room, being the largest, was planned as a resource base and training room as well as housing a parent and toddler group, physical education sessions and group activity base. Timetabling and room booking were crucial from the outset, but as an experience in truly co-operative working, everyone has gained.

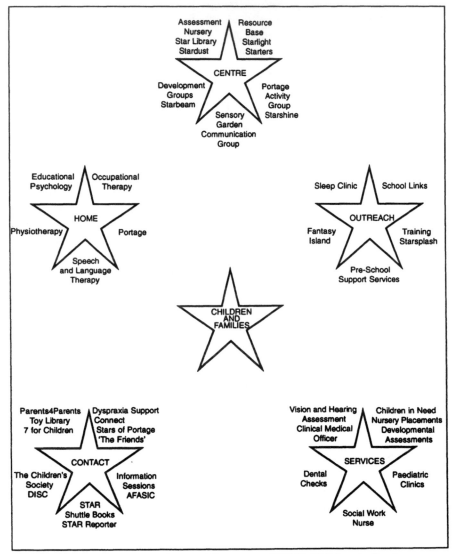

Figure 3.1 St Helens Advice and Resource (STAR) Children's Centre

Management

The Centre does not have a principal or manager, although the Head of Pre-school Service has responsibility for the building and the educational services based there. All users and staff have opportunities for involvement in planning and consultation through a series of inter-linking teams and groups. With the exception of the Portage and Outreach services operating on a supervisory basis, all groups are chaired rotationally by those attending.

Overall aims, operational policy and new directions are set by a steering group comprising representatives from:

- Parents/carers
- Community health (NHS) trust
- Hospital (NHS) trust
- Service managers
- Personal (social) services
- Voluntary Services
- Education

The group meets termly and receives an annual report. An operational team, with representatives from each discipline, meets monthly to consider new referrals, plan assessments, reviews and inter-disciplinary issues. All groups have regular planning sessions for timetabling, curricular matters and children's programmes. A Training Group addresses staff needs with all-inclusive sessions. A termly forum meeting is held, open to everyone connected with the Centre. The agenda can range from tea/coffee money to the implementation of the Code of Practice and from record keeping and ways of working to the need for more swings.

Staffing

Children recognise the individuals with whom they are involved from the photos on the wall. Parents have a point of identification and become familiar with 'official' designations from the titles below. The establishment comprises these staff, who each have varying time commitments, job descriptions, working arrangements, terms and conditions:

Administrator
Audiologist
Cleaner
Clinical Medical Officer
Consultant Community
    Paediatrician
Consultant Child and Adolescent
    Psychiatrist
Educational Psychologist/
    Head of Pre-school Service
Nurse

Ophthalmology
Orthoptist
Paediatric Continence Advisor
Physiotherapy
Portage worker
Portage support worker
Pre-school support worker
Secretary
Services for hearing and
    visually impaired
Speech and language therapy

Nursery Nurse   Starlight staff
Occupational therapy   Social worker
                                  Teacher

A comprehensive staff handbook provides information ranging from referral forms, equipment instructions and diary dates to policies on behaviour, health and safety, contact names and addresses, practices and procedures.

A journey through the stars

STAR Children's Centre provides an inter-disciplinary assessment, advice, therapy and education service for children and their families from birth until children are settled in school. An open referral system operates. Families can request help without having to await, or rely upon, a professional referral. The town centre location means that many people see young children playing and come with queries which may otherwise worry them. Increasingly grandparents call who have a concern about a child's development or, being geographically distant from their family, seek advice on a particular disability and how to help.

Children born with disabilities diagnosed pre- or peri-natally are offered a service on request. The local hospital consultant paediatricians provide information about the Centre to new parents and transmit information about children who may present with problems. However, it is often through close liaison with health visitors that initial visits are arranged to suit the parents and their personal choice of time-scale. Other children tend to emerge as particular needs become evident or parents become concerned when they do not meet developmental milestones.

A comprehensive Developmental Assessment service is offered in line with the Code of Practice, 1994 (a guidance document following the 1993 Education Act and Regulations), following similar lines to the school-based stages of assessment:

- *Stage 1* – On receipt of a referral the initial concern is recorded and an Action Plan devised. This involves gathering information about the child, with background information completed by the family or Health Visitor, taking account of the feelings and wishes of parents.
- *Stage 2* – Each assessment is individually designed taking place in a setting where the child and the family feel comfortable. Assessment may comprise any combination of the following:
  - Observation
  - Discussion with child's parent(s)/carer(s)
  - Checklist/profiles

– Testing, e.g. vision, hearing, psychometrics
– Physical examination
– Assessment in response to tuition/treatment
– Joint assessment by two or more professionals working together with recognition of each person's professional integrity.

The overriding strategy is one of inter-disciplinary working with a sharing of knowledge and skills to produce a unified child-focused strategy. Written reports are presented to the family a week before a meeting to discuss the outcome of the assessment. Parental contributions, verbally or in writing, are crucial in devising individual educational programmes stating objectives, intervention strategies, materials, people involved, frequency/timing, monitoring/assessment arrangements, help from parents at home and recording any medical requirements/health arrangements.

All children are reviewed at a maximum of 6-monthly intervals. When necessary new educational plans are formulated, for example as follows.

- *Stage 3* – Extending the previous involvement by including additional specialists' input and specific strategies for supporting the child's progress and considering, if necessary, a recommendation of Statutory Assessment of Special Educational Needs.

The home star

First contacts with children and families are usually made at home with a visitor from the Centre providing information on services, resources and facilities. This is important so that:

- Concerns, worries and anxieties can be expressed by the family on home ground.
- Information can be provided verbally and in writing.
- The visitor can make an initial observation of the child.
- An action plan can be devised with a time scale and feedback stated at the outset.
- The family have a familiar face and a named person should they subsequently attend the Centre.

All staff conduct home visits, as and when appropriate, both for assessment and treatment. The predominantly home-based service is STAR Portage service. Following an initial visit from the Supervisory a Portage Worker is allocated who visits weekly. An initial assessment period of approximately 6 weeks allows the family and Portage worker to get to know each other, observe the child's development, recording skills in motor, language, self-help, social and cognitive development.

Parents and Portage worker decide which skills are priorities for the family and child's future learning. These teaching objectives are discussed at a planning meeting with parents and professionals devising an individual education programme. Portage workers are infinitely flexible in their methods of recording, use of materials and teaching procedures. Being a regular point of contact with the family they are able to address concerns, co-ordinate appointments, provide links with other professionals and ensure that equipment is used appropriately.

The centre star

The Centre is a vibrant, lively place which, to all intents and purposes, is a nursery for young children. A wide range of groups has developed to meet need and demand. The Centre has a resource base of equipment and materials, adults' and children's libraries, the STARSHINE multi-sensory stimulation room and a sensory garden.

Star development groups

Children are placed in groups according to their age, skills and abilities; taking disability into account. Groups are varied according to current populations but generally focus on:

- Children below 18 months.
- Early learning.
- Multiple disabilities.
- Motor learning.

Activity/play sessions are co-ordinated by the Centre nursery nurse with input from education, nursing and therapy staff. Individual educational programmes and specific tuition/therapy are incorporated into the timetable.

An essential element is parental involvement and support. The first part of a session actively involves parents with mutual sharing of skills and teaching sessions in management and therapeutic techniques. The Centre nurse is available to weigh, measure and monitor children's health. Around snack time the parents are encouraged to withdraw for a drink and a chat with a Parents4Parents representative able to provide a listening ear. Parents and children have time on their own with parents having an opportunity to allow another adult to care for their child for a short period of time – not always easily achievable on account of feelings of indispensability.

Star assessment nursery

The assessment nursery caters for children, from 2.5 years to school admission, whose development is causing significant concern and whose educational needs are unclear. Through the various contributions of the inter-disciplinary team children are observed and assessed, hypotheses tested, medical investigations undertaken, response to treatment and tuition gauged. Careful consideration is given to working with parents many of whom are seeking a diagnosis or 'label' for their child.

Starlight

Many parents elect to attend this parents and toddler group rather than their local group having an awareness that their child is 'different' and not wanting to be asked why. When offered this facility an element of relief is often visible. This is a situation where no one expects parents to 'work' with their child. They can share their feelings with others. There is an element of common experience as there is some concern about their child. Frequently parents with children with disabilities and special needs are keen to leave the isolation of their own four walls knowing that they will receive a warm welcome at the Centre. As one parent of a Down's syndrome child observed, it was a 'long lonely road'.

Starters

Requests from nursery teachers for support for children who were not toilet trained led to toileting readiness checklists and parental questionnaires being devised to elicit information about the child's history, development and previous toileting attempts. Initially all children are visited at home and many successfully respond to advice on consistent toilet training. Useful guidelines have been produced by Mid-Sussex Portage Service in their booklet *Thinking about Toilet Training?* (Address in references).

Children over the age of 2 years 9 months who persistently wet can join the STARTERS group helped daily from 10.30 am to 2.45 pm. A very structured but simple routine is followed with an emphasis on the acquisition of independence skills in preparation for nursery attendance. Initially toileting is undertaken at each activity change. However, independence is encouraged so the child is soon using the toilet spontaneously. The group is run on nursery lines, with a positive atmosphere while having a high emphasis on toileting. Toileting charts are completed on a daily basis with continuous feedback to parents.

Whilst the group attained a success rate of 96% in the first 12 months it soon became evident that the context was inappropriate for those specifically with bowel problems. These children are now managed in the community through a home visiting programme.

Star communication group

This caters for nursery children whose language is their primary problem. The systematic, intensive, language-enriched experiences within the small group are complemented by age-appropriate language models at mainstream nursery.

Supported by the local branch of AFASIC (Association For All Speech and Language Impaired Children) it is frequently parents of children attending this group who appear most stressed, anxious and emotionally upset. Having had a 'normal' baby, whose early social responses and physical milestones were achieved without difficulty, parents become very concerned when their child's speech appears to be either delayed or disordered. As education looms a panic reaction often sets in. As one parental report stated:

> Our worries are that Jane will not reach her full potential unless she has specific input regarding speech and language thus enabling her to learn and cope with the academic curriculum in mainstream school. Also that the communication difficulties, if not addressed, will affect her abilities to make and sustain friendships and relationships throughout childhood and beyond.

STARBEAM

The STARBEAM (Behaviour, Education And Management) group caters for nursery children whose behaviour causes significant concern and which is impeding their ability to play appropriately and interact with others. The group's policy is to reward children for appropriate behaviour by positive reinforcement. Children have individual weekly behaviour targets, with special positive attention and reinforcement given for on-target behaviour. Inappropriate attention-seeking behaviour is actively ignored as long as it does not interfere with another child or the functioning of the group. That which cannot be ignored results in a warning and privilege withdrawal. Encouragement is constantly given to children to stay on task, follow instructions, keep hands, feet and objects to themselves and speak kindly.

An essential element is the parent support programme which parents agree to attend as an intrinsic part of their child's attendance. The positive parenting sessions make use of the *Parents and Children Series* (Webster-Stratton, 1991), a video-based course for parents, and a *Parent Resource Guide* (Canter and Canter, 1985).

Portage activity group

Having worked with children, and supported parents through weekly home visits, from shortly after birth Portage workers increasingly felt that some children need opportunities for developing their socialisation skills within a small group. Aiming to integrate children into a structured environment with others of the same age the group sets out to prepare children for nursery.

STARDUST

STAR Down's Users of Special Teaching is a weekly group for children with Down's syndrome and their parents. Sessions start with a group body awareness programme focusing on motor skills, followed by snack and individual early learning programmes to enhance cognitive awareness with specific learning difficulties addressed in line with programmes by Buckley and Bird (1993). Makaton gestures and symbols improve comprehension and increase expressive language skills. An accompanying parent support programme provides information, activities and opportunities for mutual support. Chapter 6 should also be consulted in this area of work.

STAR services

Services are provided at home, the centre or nursery. Parents appreciate a central, familiar base rather than having to attend often inconvenient and geographically distant hospitals and clinics. Paediatric, ophthalmology, orthoptic, audiology and dental sessions have nursing support and a social worker available. The allocation of Child In Need nursery placements is managed by the Centre to ensure that priority and early placement is arranged for children positively targeted as Children in Need by the Children Act (1989): 17(10)).

STAR outreach

The pre-school education service provides an outreach support service for children integrating to mainstream nurseries as well as those undergoing assessment of their educational needs. These highly qualified nursery nurses have extensive experience of children with special educational needs. All support is offered on a short-term, temporary basis via an outreach support agreement.

STARSPLASH

An innovative water/splash/aquatherapy room providing a safe, secure 'mini-seaside' which is fully accessible to young children with a wide range of disabilities.

Fantasy island

This is open to all children with a disability and their families. It is a fun resource, located in Personal Services Department and is regularly booked. The facility comprises a large soft play room with colourful mats, ball pool and cradle swing; water play room; lounge area for quiet play and relaxation as well as a safe outside play area. A maze adds interest and adventure.

Sleep clinic

Frequently health visitors ask for advice on youngsters whose parents are distressed by lack of sleep. The NFER Nelson series on *Emotional and Behaviour Problems in Young Children* (Douglas, 1988) as well as approaches from *The Sleep Book for Tired Parents* (Huntley, 1991) are used, and neighbourhood clinic sessions are arranged to give guidance and support. Often a single session will be sufficient to promote a self-help group.

School links

From the outset a Record of Achievement is commenced for each child. By school entry this conveys a wealth of information to teachers along with all the 'official' records.

Training

Training has a high priority internally for staff and externally for contacts. Individual staff keep abreast of developments within their own profession with shared opportunities for learning on topics such as, genetic counselling, aromatherapy and assessing communication skills together.

Centre staff deliver integrated courses, neighbouring services and Centres come together at regular meetings and Continuing Professional Development sessions. Many students are offered placements from a wide variety of backgrounds and disciplines.

STAR contacts

Connect

This body of parents and paid workers was set up in 1980 to improve communications between parents and paid workers and help families who have a child with a disability. Initially Connect was involved in a support group for parents and developed a handbook of useful information. Over a decade later Connect provides back-up and support, feedback on matters of concern, forthcoming events, matters of interest and new ventures.

Parents4Parents

Supported by The Children's Society, Parents4Parents are a voluntary group of parents of older children with disabilities. Having completed training in basic counselling and listening skills, these volunteers support parents of newly diagnosed children. One volunteer wrote in Information Exchange:

> Being a representative for Parents4Parents can be quite difficult when you see a parent who is experiencing your feelings from 12–13 years ago. All those memories come flooding back and you realise nothing can ease that pain and the feeling of being lost in a world where everybody seems to know where they are going. But we can say to that parent 'Yes I know that feeling, I've been there'. It does make a difference to parents to be able to talk to somebody who understands all the pressures they are under.

Stars of Portage

This small, friendly, social group for parents of children with special needs was set up in response to emotional reactions from parents when their child moved on to school and their Portage worker withdrew. Parents of children attending special schools experienced particular isolation and loneliness when their child was collected and transported to a school out of the immediate locality with few opportunities for meeting other parents informally.

Star express toy library

Providing toys and equipment for children to borrow, this parent-run facility offers a 'cuppa' and a chat.

Star reporter

A newsletter goes out on a regular basis to everyone connected with the Centre. Birthdays are celebrated, events arranged, information given,

A newsletter goes out on a regular basis to everyone connected with the Centre. Birthdays are celebrated, events arranged, information given, services spotlighted, news and views exchanged, with thank yous proliferating.

Star disc

The Disability Index of Services for Children, set up jointly by St Helens Personal Services, Education and Health, provides a register of disabled children, as required by the Children Act,1989 (Schedule 2, para 2). The accompanying information pack and regular newsletter make voluntary registration attractive.

7 for children

Fund-raising for small groups is always difficult. However a shared exercise in co-operation between seven local groups, involved with children with special needs and disabilities, has resulted in incredible income generation.

The Friends of Star Children's Centre

A registered charity supporting the Centre financially through the provision of equipment, facilities, resources, training and education.

Star shuttle books

An important link between home and Centre, the shuttle books pass messages back and forth. Parents/carers and staff communicate regularly.

Star information

As the Centre has grown and developed requests for information come from far and wide. Initially a booklet for parents and referrers sufficed. A folder of leaflets and regular sessions now disseminate information.

Key issues

Star Children's Centre has evolved from a medically based model, through a multi-disciplinary approach, to the provision of an inter-disciplinary, truly comprehensive service. Education, health, care and voluntary services work on a co-operative and creative basis, in an integrated way, with the common purpose of providing a first-class service for young children and their families.

Based within the community, the location is convenient for service users and providers. A positive atmosphere ensures that children and adults feel secure and valued. The physical environment is attractive, appropriate equipment and resources are readily available. There is time and space for everyone.

Offering a wide range of facilities and a continuum of services means that there is a high level of responsivity – from advice immediately available on a drop-in basis through to individual programme planning with different and diverse routes determined by the child's needs and family's wishes. No group or service is mutually exclusive and all services are available to all children. Each child and its family can receive a wide range of services. A package can be tried and tested for goodness of fit with adjustment made on an ongoing basis.

The Centre has a commitment to early learning, diagnosis and intervention. Planning takes place regularly and systematically with opportunities for daily feedback and ongoing record keeping. Children's progress is assessed, monitored and reviewed with special educational needs identified. Jointly negotiated learning targets for children result in integrated individual educational programmes and extensive Records of Achievement.

Partnership with parents occurs at every level and opportunity – from active membership of the Steering Group, influencing future policy and directions, to day-to-day involvement with activities. Parental contributions to their child's assessment, objective setting and future plans are highly valued. A holistic approach to the child and its family results in realistic outcomes for everyone.

The Centre is based on a team approach with all members' views and opinions having equal status. Each staff member starts from their own specific professional training/experience and, through a sound knowledge of the roles of everyone in the team, is able to co-ordinate and liaise to provide a comprehensive service. Sharing a work base, staff are able to give each other support and encouragement, reflecting on their experiences, discussing their differences and crystallising their thoughts. A combined training strategy supports professional development. Through the regular system of inter-linking meetings service users and providers are brought together. Clear policies, strategies and their implementation are shared and owned by all.

Constant appraisal, monitoring, regular review and evaluation ensures that new developments are always under consideration. The STAR system of children and families at the core, infinite flexibility and inter-disciplinary working, is responsive to changing patterns of need and the challenges that young children present to us all.

References

Canter, L. and Canter, M. (1985) *Parent Resource Guide.* Lee Canter & Associates, Behaviour Management Ltd. Suite 5, Euro House, Apex Court, Woodlands, Almondsbury, Bristol BS12 4JT.

Children Act (1989) London: HMSO.

DfE (1994) *Code of Practice on the Identification and Assessment of Special Educational Needs.* London: HMSO.

DHSS (1976) *Court Report on Child Health Services.* London: DHSS.

Douglas, J. (1988) *Emotional and Behavioural Problems in Young Children: A Multidisciplinary Approach to Identification and Management.* Windsor: NFER Nelson.

Huntley, R. (1991). *Sleep Book for Tired Parents.* London: Souvenir Press.

Buckley, S. J. and Bird, G. (1993) *The Educational Needs of Children with Down's Syndrome – a Handbook for Teachers.* Available from The Sarah Duffen Centre, Belmont Street, Southsea, Hants PO5 1NA.

Webster-Stratton, C. (1991) *The Parents and Children Videotape Series.* 1411 8th Avenue West, Seattle, WA09119.

Mid-Sussex Portage Service. *Thinking about Toilet Training?* Guidelines for Parents. Available from Mid-Sussex Portage Service, Junction Road, Burgess Hill, West Sussex RH15 0PZ.

Chapter 4

Play, Assessment and Culture

Zahirun Sayeed and Ellen Guerin

The purpose of this chapter is to provide a concise background to the relevance of play in a child's development and education. It describes a model of Play Based Assessment (PBA) which can be used by parents, carers and professionals. Observation and participatory play form the basis of this approach and have been structured to assist the assessor. This chapter explores the potential for its use with children across cultural boundaries.

Introduction

The universality of play crosses the boundaries of race, colour, language, religion and culture, but if this the case what is to be understood by play? *The Oxford English Dictionary* definition refers to occupying oneself in a game or other recreational activities. Matterson (1975) extends this idea to describe how a child learns what no one else can teach him or her. She describes play as providing a context where the world is presented in a 'manageable form, controlled quantities, pretend situations and relationships'. According to Mary Sheridan (1977:13) 'Play is the eager engagement in pleasurable physical and mental effort to obtain material benefits'. Catherine Garvey (1991:10) describes the following character-istics of play as an essential part of its definition:

- Play is pleasurable and enjoyable.
- Play has no extrinsic goal.
- Play is spontaneous and voluntary.
- Play involves some active engagement on the part of the player.
- Play has certain systematic relations to what is not play.

A short study by the authors using a small sample including nursery staff and parents in Tower Hamlets, London explored impressions of play. Play was described as :

- exploratory
- communicative
- enjoyable
- sociable
- educational
- imaginative

One member of nursery staff defined play as 'exploration – finding out about the world practising skills in an exciting, stimulating and non-threatening environment'. In response to the question 'What do you mean by play?', a parent responded 'Learning about the world and having fun'. In our view, play can be defined in terms of its overt and assumed characteristics. A child's play is elicited in response to a person or object in a context where he or she feels secure. Over time the child expends physical and mental energy for pleasure through the application of skills such as improvisation and creativity. As a state, play assumes absorption, concentration and an escape to a world that the child creates for himself or herself individually or as part of a group.

Theories of play (Figure 4.1)

An understanding of play can be derived from principal theories of developmental, cognitive, behavioural, social and educational psychology. Earlier theories emanate from an evolutionary approach leading to a within-child focus which gradually extends to the child and his or her context.

```
INSTINCT                                        BEHAVIOUR
                        PERSPECTIVES
                        ON PLAY
CHAOLOGY                                        EXPRESSION
                        EDUCATION
```

Figure 4.1 Theories of play

Nineteenth century theorists identified closely with the Darwinian school of thought. Play was described as a means of spending surplus energy, a recapitulation of ancestral behaviour and the practice of skills useful in adult life. These ideas have been refuted because they emphasise the functional characteristics of play and disregard the value of play as an enjoyable learning process.

Vygotsky (1967) underlines the role of language and communication within the child's zone of proximal development. In his view, play can act as a facilitator in helping the child to reach his or her potential – e.g.

symbolic play is recognised as crucial to the development of abstract thinking. Bandura and Walter's (1963) theory of observational learning refers to the child's play experience when the imitation of adult and peer behaviour leads to learning in the social context.

Is play a behaviour? If play is an observable response to stimuli, it should be categorised as behaviour. Play can be initiated through the introduction of a stimulus such as a preferred toy and behaviour can be sustained even when the stimulus has been removed. Play behaviour can be shaped and maintained through rewards, intrinsic or extrinsic, when applied consistently and appropriately. Claxton (1984) argues that there is no one model of learning – i.e. we can only say what a person is learning by how he or she behaves. He describes the characteristics of a good learner as one who takes time, asks questions, is not afraid of getting things wrong and enjoys finding out. He equates play with learning and how the child's 'knowing' gives him or her the confidence to know more.

Piaget (1962) identifies play as a means by which the child combines existing skills, knowledge and understanding, resulting in learning experiences. This is achieved by matching the child's cognitive development with increasingly sophisticated play activities or games. He emphasises the cognitive benefits of play, and he advocates the active participation of the child in his or her own learning. Bruner (1972) was interested in looking at play as *process led* rather than *task oriented*. Play is an approach to action not a kind of activity. Moyles (1988) also supports this view.

Freud (1922) describes all behaviour as motivated by the wishes of the individual. Play is described as a cathartic experience (Bruce, 1991), enabling the child to release anxiety and resolve future conflict. Similarly Erikson (1963) values the play experience as a way of overcoming childhood disappointments and as a preparation for the practicalities of adult life. Winnicott (1990) stresses the value of transitional objects in the development of play. Across cultures playthings such as clothing, teddies, etc. can act as a bridge between the child's dependency on his or her mother and gradual independence in his or her environment. These theories provide a framework for diagnosis and intervention through the medium of play.

Froebel, Isaacs and Macmillan as pioneers of child-centred curricula identify the 'child as a unified whole, with play as an integrated mechanism' (Bruce, 1991). Unlike the Montessori philosophy (1912) they disregarded the view of play as a preparation for adult life through the fine tuning of a child's cognitive skills. This was borne out by the Plowden Report (DES, 1967) where Piagetian style play activities were officially recognised as an essential element of early childhood education.

Chaos theory (Gleick,1988) is based on the idea that there is a non-linear relationship between process and product in all systems across a range of phenomenal principles of irregularity and uncertainty making scientific measurement impossible. In an undirected play situation the observer is never entirely sure what the child is bringing to the play situation or what he or she is getting out of it. In 'free flow play' (Bruce, 1991) the child is exploring his or her environment in a random and complex way, testing his or her ideas, experimenting with his or her feelings and relationships while simultaneously developing skills and competence.

Play as an assessment tool

What is assessment?

In recent years increasing emphasis has been placed on assessment in the Early Years geared towards National Curriculum attainment and linked to Local Education Authority resources. Assessment can be defined as the identification of the present level of a child's functioning/development through observation and interaction with an adult in order to understand and meet the child's needs. The Task Group on Assessment and Testing (TGAT; DES, 1988) states that 'Assessment is at the heart of the process of providing for children's learning'. Where children have been identified as having Special Educational Needs, early assessment is crucial to providing for the child's needs (Code of Practice, 1994). For most children assessment has become an integral part of their education. Newton (1988) suggested that pre-school assessment sets out to find out about understanding a child's functioning, learning skills, behaviour and general development with a view to facilitating and improving these. Assessment should be a process over time which enables the assessor to formulate a fuller picture of the child's strengths and weaknesses.

Why assess?

Assessment is an integral part of parents' and significant adults' interaction with the child. In the home context instinctively and continuously, parents and carers assess the child's behaviour in order to help him or her grow and develop. As the child's world radically widens to the classroom, playgroup or nursery the assessment process continues such that his or her needs can be met in different contexts. The role of the teacher or nursery staff as assessors during the early years is crucial. In general terms and more particularly in the case of children with special needs, early assessment provides a baseline from which the quality and rate of learning can be measured and progress monitored effectively.

As play is the 'spontaneous voluntary behaviour of a child' (Garvey, 1991) it provides an opportunity for adults to interact with the child, understand his or her world and support his or her learning and development in all areas.

Purposeful assessment in a structured setting can take the form of and include:

- Providing information which adults can apply to take the child's learning forward (formative and diagnostic).
- Providing evidence of the knowledge and understanding of the child (summative).
- Providing information for the adult to adapt the learning environment to suit the child (evaluative).
- Providing a medium of communication between parents and significant adults in relation to the child's progress (informative).

(DES, 1988)

Play based assessment (PBA)

Although parents and professionals from non-educational agencies have historically assessed very young children the statutory nature of Standard Assessment Tasks (SATs) for pupils aged 7 years old imply that teachers and Early Years staff need to develop skills of assessment to meet the needs of very young children in educational settings.

Along the continuum of assessment the richest information can be gathered through observation and participation (Newton, 1988). Limitations of psychometric measurements include their accessibility only to certain professionals, their low predictive value as well as cultural and contextual biases (Cummins, 1984). Other assessment methods such as interviews, reports and checklists can be used to support observational or adult directed play based assessment. According to Wolfendale (1993) assessment should:

- have a clear purpose
- be ongoing
- include parent(s)
- reflect cultural/linguistic background.

PBA = Observation and Participatory Play

Our model of PBA is an approach which combines observation and adult participation in determining a child's strengths and weaknesses. As an assessment tool it is accessible to parents and professionals in a range of contexts. PBA enables adults to conduct assessment through the child's familiar play situation. Owing to controversy surrounding norm-referenced assessment, on cultural and linguistic grounds, a criterion-referenced approach has been considered more acceptable. On the one hand, norm-referenced testing focuses on task performance, whereas criterion-based assessment explores the context of learning potential and empowers the child to cope successfully (Newson, 1993).

Table 4.1 below describes the advantages of PBA for the child and his/her assessors (parents, teachers, nursery staff and other professionals).

	Parent	Child	Teacher/ nursery staff	Other professional
Criterion referenced approach	–	–	✓	✓
Accessibility	✓	✓	✓	✓
Context embedded	✓	✓	✓	✓
Self-reinforcing	✓	✓	✓	✓
Spontaneous	–	✓	–	–
Assessment over time	✓	✓	✓	✓
Provides full picture of child	✓	–	✓	✓
Curriculum planning/monitoring	✓	–	✓	–
Culture-friendly	✓	✓	✓	✓
Suitable for all ages and ranges of ability	✓	✓	✓	✓

Table 4.1 Advantages of PBA

Observation

In PBA observation is an essential part of the assessment format. Observation schedules such as the Target Child Approach (Sylva *et al.*, 1990) structures what the assessor needs to target. Observation as an assessment technique has a universal appeal to parents and professionals because they provide useful insight into a child's learning pattern.

As part of PBA, the suggested observation schedule (Table 4.2) highlights five main areas of a child's development. The scale from 1 to 3 refers to a continuum of ability in the areas of physical, language, cognitive, social and emotional development. During the period of observation this profile can be used as a prompt and record sheet for the assessor when observing the child in solitary or group play. To use this profile most effectively the assessor may focus on each area of the child's development separately to ensure adequate detail is obtained.

This basic schedule is scaled as follows:

Weak: 1
Average: 2
Good: 3

The result obtained can be used to highlight discrete skills and/or areas of development as strengths and will indicate the need for further investigation or immediate intervention.

Areas of development	Solitary	1	2	3	Group	1	2	3
Physical	Strength				Strength			
	Mobility				Mobility			
	Balance/posture				Balance/posture			
	Whole body movement				Whole body movement			
	Ball skills				Ball skills			
	Spatial awareness				Spatial awareness			
	Hand–eye co-ordination				Hand–eye co-ordination			
	Manipulation				Manipulation			
	Others:				**Others:**			
Comments:								

Areas of development	Solitary	1	2	3	Group	1	2	3
Pre-language/ Language (first)	Imitation				Imitation			
	Gesture/pointing				Gesture/pointing			
	Eye contact				Eye contact			
	Listening (appropriate) response				Listening (appropriate) response			
	Duration of on-task behaviour				Duration of on-task behaviour			
	Babbling				Babbling			
	Naming (single words)				Naming (single words)			
	Short phrases (2/3 words)				Short phrases (2/3 words)			
	Sentences				Sentences			
	Syntax				Syntax			
	Pronunciation (with exception of accents)				Pronunciation (with exception of accents)			
	Vocabulary				Vocabulary			
	Following instructions				Following instructions			
					Plus:			
					Turn taking/sharing			
					Role play			
					Communication (non-verbally)			
					Communicating (verbally)			
					Seeking attention			
					Following instruction			
	Others:				**Others:**			
Comments:								

Table 4.2 Observation prompt sheets

Areas of development	Solitary	1	2	3	Group	1	2	3
Cognitive	Sorting (colour, shape, size)				Sorting (colour, shape, size)			
	Changing (colour, shape, size)				Changing (colour, shape, size)			
	Sequencing (colour, shape, size)				Sequencing (colour, shape, size)			
	Number concept				Number concept			
	Logical thinking				Logical thinking			
	Memory skills				Memory skills			
	Ability to pretend				Ability to pretend			
					Plus:			
					Group problem solving			
	Others:				**Others:**			
Comments:								

Areas of development	Solitary	1	2	3	Group	1	2	3
Social					Sharing			
					Turn taking			
					Imitating			
					Gesturing			
					Initiating contact			
					Leading			
					Being led in group			
					Accepting peer/adult interaction			
					Others:			
Comments:								

Areas of development	Solitary	1	2	3	Group	1	2	3
Emotional	Occupying oneself				Sharing			
	Smiling				Smiling			
	Laughing				Laughing			
	Crying				Crying			
					Hitting out			
	Others:				**Others:**			
Comments:								

Table 4.2 (continued)

Participatory play

The second component of PBA is participatory play where the assessor interacts with the child in a play situation individually or as part of a group. The adult is directly and equally involved in the child's play. In worthwhile participatory play the assessor needs to consider the following points in three essential stages:

Stage I: Pre-play
Stage II: Play
Stage III: Post-play

Stage I: Pre-Play

- Be specific about the information you will be gathering (refer to observation prompt sheet if necessary).
- Decide the number of sessions.
- Negotiate time and type of activities with other adults as far as possible.
- Decide the duration and the time.
- Decide location.
- Consider the cultural or linguistic factors.
- Familiarise yourself with the child and his or her environment.
- Decide mode of communication.
- Decide the role of other adults.
- Decide on group or individual play.

Stage II: Play

- Consider proximity to child.
- Allow child to initiate as far as possible.
- Participate at the child's level.
- Guide/lead when necessary.
- Share agenda with the child.
- Be aware of child's basic needs.
- Ensure flexibility in approach and ease of communication.
- Initiate and support pleasurable and positive interaction.

Stage III: Post Play

- Phase out gradually.
- Record (use prompt sheet if necessary).
- Structure information gathered (refer to standardised checklist if age norms are needed).
- Feedback to other adults.
- Plan next step.

Case studies

Following the completion of the observation prompt sheet the case study extracts below describe how richer information can be gathered through Stage 2 of the Participatory Play model.

Case 1

Name: Dipu.
Age: 3 years 6 months.
Ethnicity: Bangladeshi.
Current concern: Developmental delay.
Assessment focus: Imitation.

> Dipu walked towards the table where the Velcro matching shape game was laid. I modelled the activity by placing a round shape on a space on the Velcro mat. Dipu started to throw some shapes on the floor so I picked them up and repeated the activity. I gained eye contact by calling his name. I held his hand gently to allow him to feel the Velcro and focused his attention by saying 'Asho' (look) and 'Dhoro' (touch). I offered Dipu the round shape and he held it for a few seconds before sticking it on the space for squares.

Information gathered in the following areas:

- mobility
- spatial awareness
- eye–hand co-ordination
- manipulation
- imitation
- eye contact
- listening
- matching according to shape.

Case 2

Name: Sean.
Age: 4 years 9 months.
Ethnicity: White/Irish.
Current concerns: Social skills and delayed language development.
Assessment focus: Accepting adult interaction.

> Sean ran into the home corner and began to randomly arrange pots on the cooker as he pushed another child aside. I approached Sean and asked 'Can I help you?'. He ignored this remark and continued to stir the pot. I remarked 'You're stirring well'. He lost his grasp of the pot and when it fell to the floor I offered to hold it while he stirred. He found it easier and rewarding to stir while I held the pot. When I said 'I think dinner is ready' he looked at me and responded 'yeah'.

Information gathered in the following areas:
- whole body movement
- manipulation
- spatial awareness

- eye contact
- listening (appropriate response)
- ability to pretend
- sharing
- hitting out
- occupying himself.

Play and culture

Culture is a way of life which binds the thoughts, beliefs and language of a group of people in a specific context. If play is a behaviour it pre-supposes that it is affected by culture. Play cannot be separated from the experiences of the player and the context in which the play is taking place.

Winnicott (1990) offers a creative definition of culture as 'located in potential space between the human being and the environment'. Life's experiences are determined by the use of this space which is infiltrated by culture. In our role as assessors of play we must take into account this 'potential space' and experiences of the child and significant adults. 'Play is not only affected by cultural influences, it is also an expression of culture', according to Whiting and Whiting (1975).

The status of play

Universally the child's right to play has been recognised and emphasised by the International Association of the Right of the Child to Play (IPA) during a conference in Sweden in 1987. Sadly it highlighted 'society's indifference to the importance of play' with a few national exceptions including the host country.

Pre-Plowden Education trends in the 1960s and 1970s in England and Wales allowed for greater creativity in the classroom where play was often used as a learning medium. Newell (1991) describes how Article 31 from the UN Convention Report 1991 has not been given legislative status in the United Kingdom. More recently the 'back to basics' ideology has compartmentalised play and education. Fortunately some voluntary bodies such as Toy Libraries and Play Associations have managed to sustain some adult interest in play provision in schools and the community. While the ethos and cultural influence of school and family systems can influence the child's play, resource implications have become a pertinent issue.

Play, school and family culture (Figure 4.2)

The school climate and the cultural experience of the teacher can either have a positive or negative affect on the cultural appropriateness of the provision. Farver *et al.* (1995) in a comparative study of Korean American and Anglo-American pre-schoolers suggest the influence of the teacher's culture on the style of play provision. While the teacher may provide adequate materials, extended periods of time and space, his or her attitude towards play is equally significant. This study indicates that the teachers' training is superseded by his/her cultural background. Teachers also want to respond to parental expectations of what early years education should include, e.g the acquisition of academic skills is often considered to be of paramount importance.

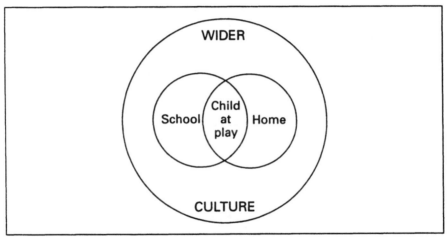

Figure 4.2 Influences on play

As the children grow and develop, their play is shaped by the home environment and its culture. When they move to the school setting they simultaneously accommodate and diversify the school culture. The multimedia and marketing culture of the 1990s has influenced what children play with rather than how they play. Consequently, teachers and school staff are important providers of play experience and assessors of play skills.

In terms of the familial factors, Swedener and John (1989) found that when parents have a positive attitude to play their children are likely to be involved in high levels of imaginative and creative play. Authors such as Feitelson (1977) suggest traditional cultures, which are based on stable beliefs, attitudes and expectations, have a negative effect on the child's imaginative play. We propose that using a model of PBA play skills should be assessed over time based on a sound understanding of the child's cultural background, early experience and current context.

Play based assessment and culture

Each time a child's play is assessed, the participants (i.e. the adult and the child) bring the elements of their own culture to bear on the situation. Therefore PBA cannot be considered free of cultural influence. The 'Tower Hamlets' study revealed that the teachers did not observe significant differences across the play of children from different cultures but on the other hand the gender difference was easily identified. This highlights the difficulties in the identification of cultural factors. If a cultural difference exists between the assessor and the player, where the assessor has a sound knowledge of the child's background and experience, the assessment process and the outcome is more meaningful.

Conclusion

The mystery surrounding a child's play and an assumed role of play in child development has always been a source of interest among parents and professionals. The theories of play provide a useful backdrop against which a child's play can be understood and used. If one accepts that play is an expression of a child's thoughts, feelings, experiences and skills, then PBA provides a holistic profile of the child. Play pervades all cultures regardless of legislative status. When knowledge of a child's culture and context are established, the observational and participatory play skills of the assessor can complete the picture of the whole child. As Educational Psychologists, the suggestions in this chapter emanate from the authors' experiences in assessing children with Special Educational Needs, particularly children in the Early Years.

Occasionally, organisational and time constraints may hinder the process of PBA. For certain professional groups who assess children in predominantly in clinical settings, the idea of assessment over time may be impractical. The suggested model of PBA has been developed on the basis of thoughts, ideas and experiences which would provide scope for research in determining its usefulness in the future.

References

Bandura,A. and Walters, R.H. (1963) *Social Learning and Personality Development.* New York: Holt, Rinehart and Winston.

Bruce, T. (1991) *Time to Play: In Early Childhood Education.* London: Hodder & Stoughton.

Bruner, J. (1972) *The Relevance of Education.* London: Allen Unwin.

Central Advisory Council for Education (England) (1976) *Children and their Primary Schools: A Report of the Central Advisory Council for Education (England).* Vol 1. London: HMSO.

Claxton, G. (1984) *Live and Learn. An introduction to the Psychology of Growth and Change in Everyday Life*. London: Harper Row.

DES (1988) *Task Group on Assessment and Testing Report*. London: Department of Education and Science.

DfE (1994) *Code of Practice on the Identification and Assessment of Special Educational Needs*. London: Department for Education.

Cummins, J. (1984) *Bilingualism and Special Education: Issues in Assessment and Pedagogy*. Avon: Multilingual Matters.

Erikson, E. (1963) *Childhood and Society*. London: Routledge and Kegan Paul.

Farver, J. M., Kim, Y.K. and Lee, Y. (1995) 'Cultural differences in Korean and Anglo-American pre-schoolers social interaction and play behaviours', *Child Development*, **66**, 1088–99.

Feitelson, D. (1977) *Cross-cultural Studies Of Representational Play*. In Tizard, B. and Harvey, D. (eds) *The Biology Of Play*. London: Spastics International Medical Publications.

Freud, S. (1922) *Beyond The Pleasure Principle. Standard Edition*. London: Hogarth Press.

Garvey, C. (1991) *Play*, 2nd edn. London: Fontana Press.

Gleick, J. (1988) *Chaology*. London/New York: Heinemann.

IPA (1987) *Creativity Through Play*. Report of the 10th Conference of the International Association for the Child's Right to Play (IPA). Stockholm: IPA.

Isenberg, J.P. and Jacobs, J.E. (1982) *Playthings as Learning Tools. A Parents' Guide*. New York: John Wiley & Sons.

Matterson, E.M. (1975) *Play With a Purpose For Under Sevens*. Harmondsworth: Penguin Books.

Moyles, J.R. (1988) *Just Playing? The Role and Status in Play in Early Childhood Education*. Milton Keynes: Open University Press.

Newell, P. (1991) *The U.N. Convention On Children's Rights in the UK*. London: National Children's Bureau.

Newson, E. (1993). 'Play based assessment in the Special Needs classroom'. In Harris, J. (ed.) *Innovations in Educating Children with Severe Learning Difficulties*. Chorley: Lisieux Hall.

Newton, C. (1988) 'Who knows me best' Assessing pre-school children. Levels of participation in a child's world', *Educational Psychology in Practice*, **3**(4), 35–39.

Piaget, J. (1962). *Play, Dreams and Imitation in Childhood*. London: Routledge and Kegan Paul.

Sheridan, M.D. (1977) *Spontaneous Play in Early Childhood from Birth to Six Years*. London: NFER Publishing Company.

Swedener, E. and John, J. (1989) 'Play in diverse social contexts: parents and teacher roles'. In Bloch, M. and Pelligini, A. (eds). *The Ecological Context of Children's Play*. New York: Ablex.

Sylva, K., Roy, C. and Painter, M. (1980) *Childwatching at Playgroup and Nursery School (Oxford Pre-school Research Project)*. Oxford: Grant McIntyre Blackwell.

Vygotsky, L. (1967) 'Play and it's role in the mental development of the child',

Soviet Psychology, **12**(6), 62–76.

Whiting, B. and Whiting, J. (1975) *Children Of Six*. Cambridge MA: Harvard University Press.

Winnicott, D.W. (1990) *Playing and Reality*. London: Routledge.

Wolfendale, S. (ed.) (1993) *Assessing Special Educational Needs*. London: Cassell.

Chapter 5

The Multidisciplinary Assessment of Under-Fives with Cerebral Palsy

Mark Fox

Introduction

Scope, formerly the Spastics Society, has for many years run a multidisciplinary assessment service. This has had a large number of different personnel over the years but essentially has always consisted of a group of professionals who have seen children and adults with cerebral palsy for a day's assessment at our centre in Fitzroy Square, London. Why do parents come from all over England and Wales for a 1-day assessment at Scope? What does it offer which is not provided by local statutory services? It will be argued in this chapter that it offers parents a reduction of uncertainty by providing expert knowledge and a process of assessment based on empowerment.

What is cerebral palsy?

Cerebral palsy has been described as follows:

> If a child has cerebral palsy it means that part of the child's brain is not working properly or has not developed normally. The affected area is usually one of the parts which control the muscles and certain body movements.
>
> (The Spastics Society; 1991:2)

Cerebral palsy is not a single or specific condition. It is more helpful to consider it as a label that describes children with a range of difficulties, owing to a range of circumstances. There is considerable variation in the extent of the affect. Children with cerebral palsy may only have one side of the body (hemiplegia) mildly affected. Or they can have all four limbs affected (quadriplegia) and find it enormously difficult even to control their slightest movements. Children with cerebral palsy also have a range of needs which are interconnected. This is best illustrated by a composite picture of some of the interconnected needs of children with quadriplegic spasticity or athetosis (common types of cerebral palsy) and the difficulties they may have in accessing the curriculum.

These children's difficulties with posture and movement mean that they are likely to have a fundamental difficulty with accessing the school and the classroom. It should be noted that they will also have a need to develop and maintain their physical skills which can be considered even more fundamental than accessing the educational curriculum.

Their difficulties with controlling movement mean that they will require appropriate positioning for functional skills: to allow them to look, to point, to write, to draw. They will also require appropriate positioning to ensure they do not develop sores or contractures and to maintain or develop their movement skills. This is a related but separate need to accessing the curriculum.

Many children with cerebral palsy also have difficulties with communication. They may well have difficulties with speech because of the motor dysfunction of their lips, tongue and palate. This motor dysfunction which leads to a speech problem is likely to be affected by their positioning which can compound or alleviate their difficulty.

In addition the motor dysfunction of their lips, tongue and palate may also cause a primary feeding problem. A child may not be able to chew and swallow. It is important for educationalists to recognise that for many children with cerebral palsy there are more fundamental needs than education in their life plan.

The child's speech difficulties may obscure other language difficulties or even a hearing loss. Speech difficulties are likely to affect significantly the teaching of key educational skills such as reading. If the child cannot say the words, feedback to the teacher about what the child has or has not learnt is limited.

The child's problems with communication may mean other significant needs are overlooked. Many children with cerebral palsy have significant visual perceptual difficulties (Davies, 1995).

Finally, of course, it should be remembered that the needs come full circle. Cerebral palsy is a medical condition used to describe the brain not working properly. This may have other physical effects including visual difficulties and epilepsy. It may well be that these sensory and physical factors compound the child's other needs.

The organisation of Scope's multidisciplinary assessments

Scope's Advisory Assessment Service is based in London but provides services to children and adults with cerebral palsy, or an associated disability, from all over England and Wales. Multidisciplinary assessment is one of the services which is provided – other work includes assessments by an individual professional, running training courses and providing advice and consultancy to statutory agencies. Last year over 200 multi-disciplinary assessments were carried out of which approximately 60 were with children under 5 years old.

Referral for multidisciplinary assessments are open and parents, professionals or Scope staff can send in an application form. These application forms are scrutinised but most are accepted if the child has some movement problem – even if it is undiagnosed as cerebral palsy. The service is promoted as an independent assessment where parents can see a range of professionals who have experience and expertise in cerebral palsy.

The multi-disciplinary assessment takes place over a day. The parents and children arrive at approximately 9.00 a.m. for a 9.30 a.m. start. During the day they are seen by a range of professionals: Speech Therapist, Occupational Therapist, Physiotherapist, Educational Psychologist and Paediatrician – and a teacher for the visually impaired if they have visual difficulties. They have an hour with each professional, and an hour and a half with the Educational Psychologist. At the end of the day, between 4.00 p.m. and 5.30 p.m. there is a panel meeting where the family meet with all the professionals together. At this meeting the issues which have arisen during the day are summarised and recommendations made. These recommendations are the actions which it is suggested that the parents try to implement locally.

After the day's assessment each professional prepares a report which summarises their views on the child. These reports are collated and the recommendations summarised. These reports and the joint recommendations are then sent directly to the parents. Copies are not sent to the local professionals but parents are encouraged to distribute them locally.

Issues of good practice

Many aspects of the multidisciplinary assessment process described above are not considered good practice (see, for example, Linder, 1990). The main areas of concern about these types of assessments are that they are:
- One-off.
- Limited in time.
- Out of context.
- Individual professional perspective.

These concerns are elaborated below.

One-off

The main argument against one-off assessments is that they simply provide a snapshot of the child at one point in time. As educationalists are usually concerned about the child's progress it is argued that a snapshot does not identify the factors which affect progress. In contrast a series of assessment can show how the child progresses over time. One-off assessments are often associated with 'testing' – which has other pejorative connotations.

Limited in time

One hour is seen as an extremely limited length of time in which to see a child. The fact that joint assessments are not usually carried out does not allow for any additional observation time. A one-off assessment means the assessor is unfamiliar with the child. They have to spend part of their session building a relationship to observe more naturalistic function.

Out of context

Contemporary theory suggests child development is interactional in so far it depends on both internal and external factors. Assessment needs therefore to take place within the contexts in which the child develops. It is considered important for the assessors to see and to understand the factors around the child which influence development.

Individual professional perspective

It is argued that different professionals only see bits of the child and do not see them holistically. This is seen to be both dysfunctional and expensive. In addition different professionals may repeat aspects of each other's assessment – 'not another three block tower'!

The espoused model for effective assessment by a range of professionals is that of a transdisciplinary approach. The transdisciplinary model is characterised by the importance of the transferring of skills across professional groups. The team members and the family undertake the assessment together and then develop a service plan based on the families' priorities. Instead of the traditional model where assessments are undertaken individually by each member of the team, members of the transdisciplinary team plan and undertake the assessment together. The assessment is functional and takes place in the child's normal environment.

The continuum from cross-disciplinary to transdisciplinary has been defined by Doyle (1993) as a method for individual professionals to check how truly transdisciplinary their work is:

1. *Low level cross-disciplinary:* Each professional individually assesses children and states goals. Team meetings do not occur. Reports are individually written.
2. *Cross-disciplinary:* Each professional individually assesses children, states goals and provides individual programme and/or therapy. Team meetings are used to share individual professional's goals for the child. Reports are individually written, and no references are made to key issues raised by other professionals.
3. *Interdisciplinary:* Each professional individually assesses child. Team meetings are used to decide on goals for the child and to share knowledge. Reports are individually written, but references are made to key elements in other professional reports.
4. *Transdisciplinary:* Professionals work jointly on assessments, sharing skills and knowledge. Team meetings are used to decide collectively on goals for the child as well as to develop interdisciplinary understanding. Reports are jointly written.

Scope's multidisciplinary assessments can best be characterised as inter-disciplinary. The one-day assessment ensures a team approach to looking at the child with cerebral palsy. It ensures a dialogue develops between the professionals which allows for shifts and developments in perspective towards a transdisciplinary approach.

Why parents come for assessment

A simple analysis of the last 10 referrals for children aged under 5 provides a snapshot of the range of issues with which parents want help.

Education: all of these parents wanted advice on education – and in particular on starting school. Sometimes parents have a very clear idea about the type of education provision which they are hoping for:

> We believe that conductive education is suitable for E. and wish to avoid a conflict (we currently have this between Peto and Bobarth techniques used by physiotherapists) that could confine or undermine her education and personal development.

Often however parents are not clear about either their child's needs or the education possibilities:

> I would like help and advice with J., especially with regard to finding the best school for his needs – I have had very little help locally.

Mobility is of concern. Therefore a school is of greater concern than perhaps with an able-bodied child, i.e. will mobility at school sacrifice the academic quality of the school?

As well as education, other concerns for parents were their child's physical development (5 out of 10) and communication (3 out of 10). Parents also had concerns about independent living skills and emotional development.

One area of concern that is frequently mentioned is diagnosis. A significant number of parents come either not having been given a diagnosis ('Confirmation of diagnosis'), or not being clear about the causes of cerebral palsy ('Why does J. have cerebral palsy?').

It is interesting to note that although queries about diagnosis are particularly prevalent with children aged under 5 they are still common from the parents of our school-age clients. Even some of our adult clients have issues about their diagnosis – including adults who have found out by accident that they have cerebral palsy!

Diagnosis is one of those areas where professionals' reassurance that it is not important does not match the reality from the parents' perspective. Professionals will argue that as long as the child's needs are met, the actual diagnosis is secondary. This may be true practically – but not emotionally where many parents require some closure on this issue. In fact it may not be true even practically as many children's needs are not met without a diagnosis. A small example of this is a recent survey undertaken by the Advisory Assessment Service in conjunction with the National Association of Paediatric Occupational Therapists. This showed that while 44% of children with a diagnosis of cerebral palsy received occupational therapy, without this diagnosis the figure dropped to 31%.

Parents appear to identify areas of Special Educational Needs (communication, physical development) but are uncertain about their significance: or more importantly, the provision which would best meet that need.

Running through all these requests for an assessment is uncertainty and anxiety on the part of the parents, which can be best summed up by one parent's comments:

Will she ever walk?

Will she ever talk?

What happens when parents are no longer there for her...?

This uncertainty is compounded by a belief that they and their child are not always going to be understood or supported, let alone empowered by those employed by statutory services.

Parents' concerns with statutory services

Parents request multidisciplinary assessments for a variety of reasons. Specific questions for assessors vary depending upon the child's needs and the services which s/he presently receives. However the parents have in common unanswered questions which they feel their local professionals are not able to resolve. There appears to be three reasons why they feel their local service cannot resolve these issues: knowledge, skills and attitude.

Knowledge: parents recognise that most of their local professionals are generalists and do not have specialist knowledge in cerebral palsy. Initially this may not be a problem but over the years as the parents' knowledge grows they become increasingly aware that the professional may not know as much about their child's cerebral palsy as they do.

Skills: tied into the above is an uncertainty of the parents whether the professional has the skills to assess their child. A professional's uncertainty about handling their child transmits to advising them on the most effective position for feeding or playing. Sometimes skills for assessing specific needs – a communication disorder on visual–perceptual difficulties – appear to be lacking. This is partly because of the limited experience many professionals have with children with cerebral palsy. More importantly because of the interconnected nature of the child's needs which makes assessment out of a multidisciplinary context extremely difficult.

Attitude: many parents recognise that the local professional is an employee of a statutory agency. Parents often believe that these professionals are therefore speaking on behalf of that agency in terms of resources. They see their child's provision dependent upon local resources rather than needs. They may also recognise that the local professional's perception is actually shaped by what is available locally. Local Education Authorities (LEAs) which have specialist Physically Handicapped schools see these as the most effective provision; a neighbouring LEA with integrated provision in Units will promote its viewpoint equally vociferously. These contradictions become very apparent at Scope when we see children from all over the country. In the same week we can see children with virtually identical needs, with very different provision, placed in radically different educational institutions. In most cases their local agencies will passionately promote their particular viewpoint if challenged. This adds to the parent's confusion, uncertain about what is right but aware of a range of options which are seemingly hidden from them.

These differences may be about education placement (integration versus segregation), physical treatment (Bobarth versus Conductive education: see Levitt (1991)), management of knees and legs (operation versus splinting) or communication (signing versus use of a communication board). All too often the professionals argue from their particular perspective and often fail to recognise the alternative perspectives with which the families (and other professionals) view the situation.

The effects of multidisciplinary assessments

Scope's Multidisciplinary Assessments' aim is to provide the family with clear recommendations to help them to move forward. Six months after the assessment the families are re-contacted. They are asked to report back on how they have used the reports from the assessment and whether the joint recommendations have been implemented.

All the parents (32 returns from children under 5) indicated last year that they were able to implement completely or partially some of these joint recommendations. From the returns it appears that approximately 80% of the recommendations are implemented. However, it is clear that this is often after considerable resistance by the statutory agencies:

> Our LEA didn't like the idea of Peter going into Mainstream school, but when it was written in the recommendations, they had to take some notice! And Peter now attends a Mainstream school. Some of the Authorities didn't take any notice but when you refer back to the report they don't like it.

The purpose of the recommendations is not simply about educational placement, only approximately 30% of the assessments give advice on the type of educational placement. Recommendations are much more likely to be about:

1. Changes in programmes (100%; 59% fully implemented).
2. Further assessment (83%; 61% fully implemented).
3. Additional resources (83%; 36% fully implemented).
4. Additional equipment (72%; 55% fully implemented).

The whole purpose of the joint recommendations is of course to ensure actual progress in development of the child: 84% of the parents felt there had actually been progress as a result of the recommendations being implemented. It is little wonder then that they felt that the assessments had been worthwhile. The areas that the parents noticed progress in were:

1. Language and communication 44%
2. Physical development   41%
3. Intellectual development   28%
4. Independent living skills   13%
5. Health   6%

Clearly, the questionnaire cannot prove if the child made progress. What it does show is that the vast majority of the parents of children aged under 5 believed that their child had actually made progress in their development as a result of the recommendation being implemented. This clearly has a very empowering effect on the parent. It is something that they have done for their child that has actually made a difference.

The value of multidisciplinary assessments

There are two underpinning reasons why parents seem to value Scope's multidisciplinary assessments:

- Seeing a range of professionals with expertise in cerebral palsy.
- Receiving an empowering view of their child.

These two reasons appear paradoxical because it can be argued that the expert professional model disempowers parents. However, it is how that expertise is used that disempowers, or empowers.

For many parents of children with cerebral palsy there is a series of interconnected needs. All too often they are not helped to see the holistic picture of their child where they can understand the interconnection between the needs and provision, treatment or resources which they are offered.

One of the major powers of Scope's multidisciplinary assessments is seeing a range of professionals on the same day. The parents over the day gradually build up a picture, which makes sense to them, of the issues with which they are concerned. At the final panel meeting they have the chance to hear the whole picture articulated and to question discrepancies in perspective. It is clear that often this is the first time that the parents have had an opportunity to discuss the connection between the needs outlined by the paediatrician and a physiotherapist or between an educational psychologist and a speech and language therapist. It is hearing these experts' opinions and seeing the whole picture which the parents find helpful.

Receiving an empowering view of their child

As well as this expert model of cerebral palsy where the child's needs are analysed and interconnected there is another model which is at the heart of the assessments. For many parents the real issues about having a child with cerebral palsy are the politics about having their needs met. Politics in this sense is about how power is used and decisions made by professionals.

It has been recognised for some time that professionals can play three different roles with parents: the expert, transplant or consumer role (Cunningham and Davies, 1985). In recent years two other models have been described (Hall and Hill, 1996): the social network model, and the empowerment model.

The social network model

This model emphasises that the child is part of a social network which has a powerful influence on their development. There are social factors such as housing and unemployment which have a significant effect on the child's needs. Parents will also use their social network for information and support as much as professionals. Professionals need to be aware of the influence of the social factor and use it to assist families in setting priorities for children.

The empowerment model

This model emphasises the empowerment of parents. It emphasises the importance of the parents' ability to plan organise and carry out the decisions that they think are right for their families.

The empowerment model is closely tied with a consumer or client perspective of services. The client, the person with cerebral palsy, or their parents if they are young, have a range of options in terms of services and resources. The professional basis for choosing one option rather than another is limited. The family have needs too and they have a right to make choices to satisfy some of their needs.

Fundamental to the empowerment model is a phenomenological perspective. This is a recognition that a family's needs are not fixed but are always and continually modified by their perception of their experiences. Parents' expectations influence what they consider needs. These expectations are moulded by social circumstances of the individual – including where they live and the services which are presently available to them.This means that at different times and in different circumstances parents define their needs very differently according to what they learn is available and possible. Needs in other words is a relative concept. In recent years there has been a growing voice of more appropriate models for disability. This is central to the phenomenological perspective. As Finkelstein persuasively argues in *The Psychologist* letters (August 1996:342):

> Similarly the able-bodied obsession with walking seems to prejudice objecti-
> vity in developing an understanding of disability. When able-bodied people
> don't walk (say to and from their place of employment) they may not only
> exhibit this behaviour 'because of a combination of lack of intention to walk

and the belief that they cannot walk' that distance but simply because they can use an able-bodied mobility aid like a car, bus or train. The lifestyles of disabled people cannot be interpreted as a deviance from able-bodied lifestyles ... any more than the lifestyle of women or people from ethnic minorities can be adequately interpreted as deviations from ... men or Anglo-Saxons.

The needs of a child with cerebral palsy cannot be adequately defined objectively by a professional. Nor can they be adequately defined by a parent in isolation from an expert knowledge base about cerebral palsy.

One helpful way of reconciling the expert and phenomenological perspective is the framework known as Johari's Window (Jongeward and Seyer, 1978). This shows the assessment of needs is a two-way process (Figure 5.1).

	Known by Professional	Not known by Professional
Known by Parent	Open Need	Hidden Need
Not known by Parent	Closed Need	Unknown Need

Figure 5.1 Johari's Window

The open quadrant refers to things which the parents know are needs which are also known by the professional, e.g. problems of mobility.

The closed quadrant refers to things that the professional knows (about cerebral palsy) which the parent does not know, e.g. age factors which affect mobility.

The hidden quadrant refers to things that the parent know about the needs but are not known by the professional, e.g. the problems of toileting using the wheelchair.

The unknown quadrant refers to things that neither the parent or professional know about the child's needs, e.g. changes in design of an electric wheelchair.

Assessment serves little purpose if it simply confirms what parents already know. The size of the open quadrant needs to be enlarged by giving the parent 'closed' information about cerebral palsy and ensuring that their 'hidden' perspective on disability is heard. The model shows how the parents and the professionals each have information which when combined provide a clearer picture of the issues which this child, in this family, will face growing up.

Until the parents are truly treated as clients their perspective will always be considered as unimportant. It is only when they are given buying power in the economic sense of the word that professionals will truly listen to them as clients. Ultimately there may need to be a complete split in education, health and social services between purchasers and providers. Assessment of needs may have to be genuinely independent of the provision and resources to meet these needs. In this way the parents' confidence in the professionals will once again return – especially if this is married to genuine expertise in their child's disability.

References

Cunningham, C. and Davies, H. (1985) *Working with Parents: Frameworks for Collaboration*. Milton Keynes: Open University Press.

Davies, M. (1985) 'Beyond physical access for students with cerebral palsy'. *The Psychologist,* 8(9), 401–404.

Doyle, T. (1993) *Multidisciplinary Assessment of Children under Five with Cerebral Palsy*. Unpublished MSc dissertation, Psychology Department, University of East London.

Finkelstein, V. (1996) 'Whose model of disability?' *The Psychologist* 9(8), 342.

Hall, D. and Hill, P. (1996) *The Child with a Disability*. Oxford: Blackwell Science.

Jongeward, D. and Seyer, P. (1978) *Choosing Success: Transactional Analysis on the Job*. Chichester: Wiley.

Levitt, S. (1991) *Treatment of Cerebral Palsy and Motor Delay*. Oxford: Blackwell Science.

Linder, T. (1990) *Transdisciplinary Play Based Assessment – A Functional Approach to Working with Young Children*. Baltimore: Brookes.

The Spastics Society (1991) *What is Cerebral Palsy?* London: The Spastics Society. (Now Scope)

Further reading

Cornwall, J. (1996) *Choice, Opportunity and Learning – Educating Children and Young People who are Physically Disabled*. London: David Fulton Publishers.

Chapter 6

The Special Educational Needs of Children with Down's Syndrome

Stephanie Lorenz

Introduction

This chapter aims to give a general introduction to Down's syndrome and its effects in young children. Consideration is given to a range of factors that are likely to have a bearing on the provision of an appropriate educational regime. Attention is drawn to some of the most recent research on the development of language and memory skills, on the teaching of reading and on the benefits of inclusive school placement. Examples are offered from the author's recent experience and some conclusions reached about the best way forward for this particular group of children. Further information on topics covered in this chapter can be found in *Children with Down's Syndrome* (Lorenz 1998).

Down's Syndrome and its effects

Down's syndrome is a genetic condition, caused by a failure in cell division, which results in the baby having a third copy of chromosome 21. Babies can generally be recognised at birth by their distinctive facial features, as well as by other physical signs.

Heart defects are relatively common, but are generally operable. Small canals in the middle ear and an increased risk of respiratory infection lead to a higher than average incidence of conductive hearing loss, while delays in the development of the auditory system can lead to sensori-motor problems.

Hearing difficulties are generally treated by draining off excess fluid and inserting 'grommets' or, increasingly, by the fitting of hearing aids. This latter course is often favoured for even mild losses, as 'grommets' frequently fail to fit the characteristically small ear canal. Visual problems are even more prevalent, and many young children with Down's syndrome are prescribed spectacles.

Poor muscle tone is very common in babies with Down's syndrome and this leads to delayed motor milestones and a tendency to clumsiness. Slack muscles in the tongue and mouth, combined with obstructed nasal passages, lead many young children with Down's syndrome to become mouth breathers and to protrude their tongue. However, this tendency can be controlled by exercise and encouragement. While all children with Down's syndrome show some delay in their development, they vary widely in their learning ability. These differences may be genetic, caused by the specific combination or expression of the genes on the 21st chromosome. They may be due to untreated, uncorrected or undiagnosed secondary medical conditions. They may be due to the presence of an unrelated disability such as autism or epilepsy or they may be due to environmental factors:

Paul appeared to develop more slowly than other children with Down's syndrome. His play was solitary and he avoided the company of other children. Language failed to develop and he showed no interest in acquiring signing skills. Play was limited and he showed a preference for stereotyped activities including twirling and flapping. Observation over a period of time indicated that in addition to having Down's syndrome, Paul was also autistic.

Nancy was born prematurely and exhibited a range of difficulties, including severely delayed development, partial sight and epilepsy. These appeared unrelated to her Down's syndrome and were attributed to substance abuse by her mother during pregnancy.

On starting school at 5, the most able children with Down's syndrome are often functioning near an average level for their age . At the other end of the ability range, children with Down's syndrome can be found who have severe difficulties. Lorenz (1984) tested 77 children on the Stanford-Binet scale at 5–6 years of age and found an IQ range from 10 to 92, with a mean of 44. While children with Down's syndrome were considered ineducable until 1970, it now appears that a significant proportion of children with the syndrome experience only moderate learning difficulties.

For many children with Down's syndrome, communication presents particular problems. This may be due to recurrent middle ear infection and consequent hearing loss, to poor muscle tone in and around the mouth and face, or to limited cognitive skills, particularly in the area of auditory memory. These difficulties can lead, in turn, to delayed speech, poor articulation, dysfluency or word finding problems:

Martin walked independently soon after his second birthday but failed to produce any clear words until he was four. While his non-verbal skills are excellent he continues to have significant language difficulties.

Russell is a lively and outgoing young man. At 6 he is able to speak in short sentences and continually asks questions. However, unless you know him well, you may find him hard to understand, because of his poor articulation.

While each child with Down's syndrome is an unique individual, with his or her own combination of strengths and weaknesses, some common threads in development can be identified. Work by Faulkener and Lewis (1995) suggests that development in children with Down's syndrome is different from that of normally developing children and not merely delayed.

Studies by a range of authors (e.g. Bower and Hayes, 1994), have found particular delays in the development of short-term auditory memory skills, significantly greater than in other children with an equivalent degree of developmental delay, although their performance on visual memory tasks was equivalent. These deficits may be due to a neurological delay, or to a failure to develop appropriate memory strategies (Broadley and MacDonald, 1993). Not only do young children with Down's syndrome fail to develop these particular skills, but there is also evidence that they make poor use of skills that are developed. Wishart (1993) concludes that children with Down's syndrome are less well motivated than other learners of a similar developmental level and tend to adopt behavioural strategies which undermine the progress of their learning:

Jenny and Naomi are two little girls of similar age who attend the same school. While developmentally, Jenny is more advanced, her obstructive behaviours are interfering with her learning. On the other hand, Naomi continues to respond positively and so makes steady progress.

Parents may find that social behaviours are used by the child to distract adult attention and so avoid tasks seen as too difficult, too easy or too much trouble. The characteristic 'stubbornness' of many children with Down's syndrome may reflect this tendency which may also explain the apparent 'plateauing' of development in later years.

Certainly it is an issue that needs to be addressed in early intervention and in preschool programmes, as is the evidence furnished by Wishart (1996), that young children with Down's syndrome quickly learn to depend on the support of others in learning contexts, even when that support is not needed.

Early intervention

For all children, particularly those least able to compensate, the quality of their early environment may be critical in determining later learning potential. Nevertheless, objective evaluation of intervention programmes for young children with Down's syndrome is difficult to find, as appropriate control groups are rarely available.

Wishart (1996) notes that early intervention programmes are often given the credit for the higher levels of competence shown by young children with Down's syndrome today. However, this undoubted improvement may in fact be due to better management of health problems, greater access to everyday experiences and the more positive attitude of parents and teachers.

While a high proportion of the children in receipt of early intervention programmes are those with Down's syndrome, no differential strategies, which work from the specific profile of skills displayed, have been developed for this group. Lorenz (1984) and Sloper *et al.* (1986) note that gains made during early intervention are often relatively short lived and children receiving later stimulation soon catch up. So where should the focus for early intervention programmes be placed? Work on the development of communication skills in young children with Down's syndrome indicates that for many, the acquisition of foundation skills such as reciprocal gaze and turn-taking are the key to successful interaction.

Since many young children with Down's syndrome are slow to develop these skills (Rondal, 1996), they can usefully be incorporated into a home-based teaching programme. By increasing the sensitivity of parents to their child's responses, e.g. by encouraging them to give their child more time to respond, everyday opportunities can be capitalised upon and development fostered within normal settings.

While up to 75% of young children with Down's syndrome may show delays in speech development, they commonly have greater strengths in visual perception and in motor development. Consequently, they frequently find it easier to learn to sign than to speak.

For the majority of young children with Down's syndrome, a total communication approach, utilising a signing system such as Makaton, together with spoken English, has proved to be the most effective way into verbal communication. Despite many parents' fears that the introduction of signing will delay speech acquisition, research fails to support this position:

> James was slow to develop speech, although his understanding was good. He was introduced to Makaton by his speech therapist and soon acquired a range of signs which he used to communicate. However, speech was also developing and by the age of five when he started school, it was clear that he no longer needed the support of signs.

To encourage optimal language development in young children with Down's syndrome, a programme of frequent structured activities is apparently required. These are often best carried out by the parent, in the home, where the child feels most comfortable. However, because of the specialised nature of the skills to be taught, professional guidance and support from a speech and language therapist, experienced in work with young children, is essential.

Work with school-aged children (Philps, 1993) indicates that merely exposing children with Down's syndrome to peers with a high level of verbal competence may be counter-productive. This would appear to be equally true with pre-school children.

Instead, the child with Down's syndrome needs to be given opportunities to take the lead or to practise skills with others at a similar level of language development. This can be done by means of specialised small group work, or alternatively, in a one-to-one setting, with an adult aware of the appropriate level of demand required.

Current literature suggests that the development of memory and language skills is of importance for later learning in children with Down's syndrome. Thus, any early intervention strategies that foster these skills clearly merit serious consideration. A significant and growing body of research evidence now supports the view that not only can young children with Down's syndrome be taught to read from around two or three years of age, but that, in so doing, their memory and language skills are enhanced (Laws *et al.*,1995):

> Jane developed reading skills before she started school. By six she had a Reading Accuracy Score of 7 years 8 months and a Comprehension Score of 7 years 2 months. Auditory memory skills were around a 6 year level and she was able to ask and answer questions as well as speaking about future and past events.

In developing more appropriately focused early intervention strategies for children with Down's syndrome, it is important that attention is paid to more than the content of structured programmes. As Wishart (1996) has shown in her work, intervention can lead to 'switching out' or 'learned helplessness'. These avoidance strategies, established in the early years, can persist throughout life and substantially interfere with future learning.

In developing techniques to avoid these problems, thought needs to be given to motivation and to the responses of adults to avoidance strategies which may be seen as amusing. It is also important that early intervention programmes address the development of independence in the young child, to avoid later reliance on structured input, regular prompting and high levels of social reinforcement.

Experience of children with full-time support in school would suggest that adult dependency, once established, can inhibit future learning to a significant degree.

By rethinking the content and the presentation of early intervention programmes for young children with Down's syndrome, we may be able to improve learning outcomes. However, as Guralnick (1996) suggests, it might be better to move the emphasis away from the acquisition of specific language and cognitive skills to focus instead on the development of peer-related social competence.

To develop social skills, it appears important from an early age to provide inclusive social settings for young children with Down's syndrome, beyond the family network, in which skills can be practised in the company of more competent peers (Buysse and Bailey, 1993). Guralnick (1990) suggest that even in such settings, peer-related social competence in young children with Down's syndrome is likely to be deficient, unless particular thought is given to overcoming difficulties resulting from limited cognitive skills and emotional regulation.

Children with Down's syndrome are likely to need help in understanding social rules and accepted sequences of everyday behaviour, if they are to gain acceptance into the peer group. Because of their particular difficulties, attention needs to be paid to intervention approaches involving social imitation and the use of predictable play sequences in a range of social contexts.

Assessment and placement of pre-school children

While for many psychologists, the assessment of pre-school children is still based largely on observation over time in a range of settings, a growing number are reverting to the administration of standardised tests. Although many practitioners would express severe reservations about the reliability of such measures for any pre-school child, results need to be interpreted with particular caution in the case of children with Down's syndrome.

Extensive work by Wishart and her colleagues (e.g. Wishart and Duffy, 1990) has indicated that performance in this group is particularly erratic with, in one study, test–retest scores increasing in 74 instances but decreasing in 91, with children aged from 6 months to 4 years unwilling or unable to reproduce a previously successful performance. This, they suggest, may be due to an instability in learning and poor consolidation of skills, or to motivational factors such as a failure to engage with the task.

Certainly as a reliable predictor of successful mainstream placement, IQ appears to be one of the least useful measures. Yet evidence from the

SEN Tribunal would suggest that some LEAs still rely heavily on psychometric assessment in the categorisation of young children with Down's syndrome.

While there is no evidence to suggest that the range of abilities displayed by children with Down's syndrome in different areas of the country varies significantly, differences in placement practice are enormous. In some LEAs, at least 80% of 5 year olds with Down's syndrome are placed in the mainstream (Bird and Buckley, 1994; Lorenz, 1995). In others, such placements are rare and occur only where parents are prepared to fight LEA recommendations.

Experience over a number of years indicates that children with quite significant learning difficulties can attend their local mainstream school and do well. An increasing body of evidence (e.g. Casey *et al.*,1988; Lorenz *et al.*,1985; Sloper *et al.*,1990) points to the fact that children with Down's syndrome placed in mainstream schools do at least as well, if not better than special school peers on a range of academic measures. Parents and teachers report gains in social skill, increased independence and the development of friendship patterns.

> Jordan attended a special school part-time and a mainstream school for the rest of the week. When it was his birthday his mother invited all the children in both classes. While all the local mainstream children came to his party, no-one came from the special school.

While factors such as delayed language development, inappropriate behaviours or the absence of toilet training are often used as reasons to deny children with Down's syndrome access to the mainstream, all can be successfully overcome with appropriate training and support for school staff. Few problems presented by young children with Down's syndrome, are unique and most are part of the normal experience of early years staff. Yet, when combined with the label of Down's syndrome they can be seen as beyond the range of expertise of even the most competent teacher.

In trying to quantify the factors that are likely to increase the probability of successful mainstream placement, it is necessary to look well beyond the child. Petley (1994), in her study of ten children placed in local mainstream schools, stresses the importance of the school's attitude towards the child. The author's experience would support this view, for when problems arise, as they inevitably will, one school will address them directly while another will see them as evidence of failure and seek alternative placement.

To avoid such difficulties, it is important that schools are provided with as much information as possible before the child starts, as well as with ongoing support as the placement continues. Mainstream staff need to know what is considered to be 'good' progress for a child with Down's syndrome and when they should start becoming worried. Parents should share with schools their hopes and expectations and in this way reduce the perceived pressure for the child to keep up academically with his or her peers:

> Robert was doing really well in his mainstream school. His parents were very happy with his progress as was his support assistant. Yet his Headteacher continually informed visiting professionals that they were not meeting his needs. When questioned, he was unable to define which needs were not being met and at Tribunal, the appropriateness of his placement was confirmed.

Under most circumstances, a child starting school at nursery age is more likely to succeed than one starting at 5 or later. In a nursery, there are likely to be a wide range of activities in which children with Down's syndrome can demonstrate their skills. Pressures to deliver a set curriculum and assess its outcomes are fewer and, in general, other children are more accepting of individual differences. Most nursery staff are used to a wide ability range and use existing skills as a basis for the development of individual programmes.

Once a child is accepted into a nursery and staff have had time to build a relationship with the child and the parents, transition into school is likely to be easier. There is also the opportunity to consider keeping the child down for an additional year. Inclusive practice in the UK tends to favour the retention of children with Down's syndrome with a younger peer group.

In many instances, if decisions are made in the early years and the child remains with the same peers, this can be advantageous. Many children with Down's syndrome are smaller and more immature than their peers. Extra time in the nursery or in reception can give the child time to consolidate basic skills before moving on to a more academic curriculum. However, caution needs to be exercised when children are kept back in successive years, in a search for the elusive 'curriculum match' as relationships, which are slowly developing, may be disrupted:

> Richard was initially placed in the nursery of his local school with his peers. However, when they moved up he stayed down an extra year, moving into school with the new group. While this could have worked, had he remained with those children, he was kept down for 2 further years. At Tribunal, the LEA used his social isolation as a reason for recommending special school placement. The Tribunal, however, confirmed his mainstream placement.

Another common practice is to arrange a split placement with the child attending a special school for part of the week and a mainstream school for the remainder. While some parents feel this represents the best of both worlds, it can also be problematic and is generally not recommended.

Where the mainstream school only has the child for 1 or 2 days, there is a tendency for them to view their role as providing 'social integration', leaving the special school to determine the academic content of the child's programme. Thus, opportunities for the child with Down's syndrome to learn alongside normally developing peers are often missed. Teaching and behavioural strategies in the two settings can also be very different and, without joint planning, can lead to confusion for the child:

> John was a little boy who had initially started attending a special school when he was 2 as no other provision was available. When he reached 4, his parents asked for a mainstream placement and he was offered 2 days a week in his local school. However, he found this very difficult and was badly behaved on a Thursday when he changed schools. By Friday afternoon, he settled into the mainstream setting and his behaviour improved just in time for his return to the special school on Monday.

To overcome these problems, any joint placement requires very careful planning and collaborative working between the two schools. Even then, the major problem of social disjunction is difficult to overcome. Opportunities for building relationships in either setting will be reduced and children in the mainstream are unlikely to perceive the child who only attends part time as belonging to the class. Placement in a unit or resource attached to a mainstream school can have a similar effect on the development of relationships and social acceptance, if careful thought is not given to opportunities for informal contact between mainstream and unit children:

> Sonia attends a Unit attached to a mainstream infant school. The Unit is in a separate building across the playground. Although she goes into school assembly with her class and joins in some lessons, she has no mainstream friends and no one talks to her as she walks across the playground to the Unit each day.

Conclusions

In considering best practice in meeting the needs of young children with Down's syndrome, it seems clear that there is much to be gained both from home-based early intervention and from inclusive school placements. However, a lot more thought needs to be given to the particular difficulties experienced by these children and ways in which existing programmes can be focused to address them more directly.

If, as research now suggests, the development of children with Down's syndrome is different from that of other groups and not just delayed, then it would be a major omission on our part if we failed to utilise this knowledge in developing appropriate interventions.

References

Bird, G. and Buckley, S. (1994) *Meeting the Educational Needs of Children with Down's Syndrome*. Portsmouth: University of Portsmouth.

Bower, A. and Hayes, A. (1994) 'Short-term memory deficits and Down's syndrome', *Down's Syndrome: Research and Practice*. **2**(2), 47–50.

Broadley, I. and MacDonald, J. (1993) 'Teaching short-term memory skills to children with Down's syndrome', *Down's Syndrome: Research and Practice*, **1**(2), 56–62.

Buysse, V. and Bailey, D. (1993) 'Behavioural and developmental outcomes in young children with disabilities in integrated and segregated settings', *The Journal of Special Education*, **26**, 434–61.

Casey, W., Jones, D., Kugler, B. and Watkins, B. (1988) 'Integration of Down's syndrome children in the primary school', *British Journal of Educational Psychology*, **58**, 279–86.

Faulkener, D. and Lewis, V. (1995) 'Intervention: Down's syndrome and autism'. In Bancroft, D. and Carr, R. (eds) *Influencing Children's Development*. Oxford: Blackwell.

Guralnick, M. (1990) 'Social competence and early intervention' *Journal of Early Intervention*,**14**, 3–14.

Guralnick, M. (1996), 'Future directions in early intervention'. In Rondal, J., Perera, J., Nadel, L. and Comblain, A. (eds) *Down's Syndrome, Psychological, Psychobiological and Socio-Educational Perspectives*. London: Whurr Publishers.

Laws, G., MacDonald, J., Buckley, S. and Broadley, I. (1995), 'The influence of reading instruction on language and memory development in children with Down's syndrome', *Down's Syndrome Research and Practice*. **3**(2), 59–65.

Lorenz, S. (1984) *Long Term Effects of Early Intervention in Children with Down's Syndrome*. Unpublished PhD, University of Manchester.

Lorenz, S. (1995) 'The placement of children with Down's syndrome', *British Journal of Special Education*. **22**(1), 16–20.

Lorenz, S. (1998) *Children with Down's Syndrome*. London: David Fulton Publishers.

Lorenz, S., Sloper, P. and Cunningham, C. (1985) 'Reading and Down's syndrome', *British Journal of Special Education*, **12**(2), 65–7.

Petley, K. (1994) 'An investigation into the experiences of parents and headteachers involved in the integration of primary aged children with Down's syndrome into mainstream school' *Down's Syndrome: Research and Practice*, **2**(3), 91–7.

Philps, C. (1993) *A Comparative Study of the Academic Achievement and Language Development of Children with Down's Syndrome Placed in Mainstream and Special Schools*. Unpublished M.Phil., University of Wolverhampton.

Rondal, J. (1996) 'Oral language in Down's syndrome'. In Rondal, J. *et al.* (eds) *Down's Syndrome, Psychological, Psychobiological and Socio-Educational Perspectives*. London: Whurr Publishers, pp.99–119.

Sloper, P., Glenn, S. and Cunningham, C. (1986) 'The effect of intensity of training on sensori-motor development in infants with Down's syndrome', *Journal of Mental Deficiency*, **30**, 149–62.

Sloper, P., Cunningham, C., Turner, S. and Knussen, C. (1990) 'Factors relating to the academic attainments of children with Down's syndrome' *British Journal of Educational Psychology*, **60**, 284–98.

Wishart, J. (1993) 'Learning the hard way: avoidance strategies in young children with Down's syndrome', *Down's Syndrome: Research and Practice*, **1**(2), 47–55.

Wishart, J. (1996) 'Learning in young children with Down's syndrome'. In Rondal, J. *et al.* (eds) *Down's Syndrome, Psychological, Psychobiological and Socio-Educational Perspectives*. London: Whurr Publishers, pp.81–99.

Wishart, J. and Duffy, L. (1990) 'Instability of performance on cognitive tests in infants and young children with Down's syndrome', *British Journal of Educational Psychology*, **59**, 10–22.

Chapter 7

Early Years: The Integration of the Visually Impaired Child

Mary Burke

Introduction

I have been the London Borough of Hackney's Peripatetic Teacher of the Visually Impaired for nearly 10 years. In this chapter I attempt to describe my work with young children and their families from my initial involvement through to their integration into mainstream nursery education.

I recently arranged for a 19-year-old blind former pupil of mine, who is about to enter university, to visit a Hackney nursery, with her newly acquired guide-dog. The nursery has admitted visually impaired children for some years and needless to say the children were fascinated by the abilities of the dog, resulting in one 3 year old asking if he could sing as well! While incidents like this are memorable, it is also invaluable for staff, and a blind child's parent, to meet a young person who has gone through the education system as a visually impaired child and has done well.

The inclusion of any child with special needs in mainstream education is not static but is continually changing and developing. Once a visually impaired child is in a mainstream setting that is deemed to be successful it would be easy to become complacent. However, awareness raising sessions are vital.

The term 'visual impairment' covers the whole range of visual difficulties from varying degrees of partial sight through to blindness. During the years I worked in a special school many of the children I taught had problems in addition to their visual impairment such as hearing loss, cerebral palsy and physical disabilities. In the early 1980s, owing to the growing emphasis on schools providing for their own children with special needs, schools which had traditionally catered for blind and partially sighted pupils were becoming more generic in their intake; this meant a subsequent growth of experience for the teachers involved which has been extremely useful in my present role, since half my caseload is made up of children who have additional problems.

Referrals and appointments

Children are referred to me through a number of channels, but mainly via the Donald Winnicott Centre child development clinic at the Queen Elizabeth Hospital, Moorfields Eye Hospital or one of the local hospitals which the child has attended since birth.

If a child is referred via the Donald Winnicott Centre there is automatically a multi-agency approach. Information from a multitude of medical professionals is invaluable in drawing up a full picture of a child's needs.

Referrals are made with a parent or carer's* knowledge. I generally contact parents directly by letter, explaining my role and offering a choice of two appointments. By the time I make personal contact I have a medical report and full details of the child's visual condition. Many parents need the opportunity to talk through their child's medical history. Sometimes they have a limited understanding of their child's impairment, either because they were too distraught at the time of diagnosis, or the consultant did not think it necessary or appropriate to give detailed information.

My first meeting with the family is undoubtedly of paramount importance if the relationship is to be a positive one. Parents may have had contact with a number of professionals before me and may be feeling overwhelmed. Adding to a family's stress would be counterproductive at this time. Conversely I may be the first professional to contact a family since the child was brought home from hospital, and may be a welcome interruption to feelings of isolation.

The diverse nature of the families visited requires sensitivity and awareness of cultural and religious issues within the home, including the use of materials and the advice given. It may also necessitate the use of an interpreter. Flexibility is vital in order to accommodate an individual family's requirements. Not all families and cultures share the educational professional's attitude towards toys and our perception of their value. An awareness and acceptance of these differences is essential.

An answering machine linked to a direct line in my office on which parents can leave messages of a private and personal nature not only ensures confidentiality but means that they can always make contact in times of crisis.

---

*For the sake of convenience I have used the term 'parent' throughout to refer to either parent or any other main carer. I have adopted a convention of using feminine references to adults and masculine ones to children.

Working with parents or carers

The most important component of any child's development is the relationship between the child and the main carer, usually the mother. A child with reduced vision or no vision may have difficulty in developing self-awareness. If there is no strong bond between a child and parent during early infancy the child will inevitably find it more difficult to gain a sense of self and a feeling of the importance of self in relation to others.

Gauging what it is that a family most needs and wants is essential. Through experience I have learnt to accept the many ways that parents react to my involvement. It is pointless having pre-conceived ideas about what I am going to do. If parents are angry or aggressive this is often connected with the misplaced guilt they may be feeling about their child's difficulties or perhaps because of the way they have inadvertently been treated by family, friends or hospital staff. A parent may not be feeling fully supported by her partner or, if she is a single parent, she may be feeling overwhelmed. Sometimes a child may have a rare condition, in which case putting families in touch with each other can reduce feelings of isolation. I facilitate the contact and leave parents to get in touch themselves. Ability to focus on the visually impaired child's needs may be further complicated by the presence of siblings. To some extent these issues have to be acknowledged before a parent can listen and assimilate information. The issue of confidentiality may also need to be raised; vulnerability and family pressures might make it impossible for parents to feel able to discuss their child's impairment openly.

At an appropriate time, discussion takes place around the subject of activities and management of the child in general. While talking and listening to the parent, I might also be holding and playing with the child. Depending on the stage of the child's development I might be trying to encourage 'reaching' for toys – something that many visually impaired children find difficult. Many toys are made from the same kind of plastic and differ very little from each other in tactile quality, taste or smell. Parents need encouragement to provide a variety of textured toys including those made from wood and metal; real objects such as kitchen utensils (a favourite with all children), a shoe, a cup, a spoon or a hairbrush can teach a visually impaired child more than any commercially produced toy. Fruit such as oranges smell delicious, feel interesting and roll along the floor really well, offering more sensory stimulation and encouraging a child to explore for a longer period of time. In playing with everyday objects the child is becoming familiar with their properties.

As well as giving information about the development of the blind child and discussing the child's progress, I sometimes use an assessment/skills inventory such as the Oregon Project (Jackson Education Service District,

1978) which not only assesses the child's developmental level in six categories but also selects appropriate teaching goals, and records the child's acquisition of new skills. Some parents enjoy this way of working.

A totally blind child with no other impairment is almost certainly going to need to learn braille. Discussing this with parents at an early stage is useful, not only so that they become accustomed to the idea, but to enable them to make arrangements to learn braille themselves if they wish. While a policy of the sooner the better might be apt, everyone has to come to a decision at a time that is right for them.

Choosing an educational placement

Parents are usually keen for their child to be in mainstream education at nursery level, even if they are thinking about special school at a later stage. I have rarely had to discuss the benefits of going to a local mainstream nursery as opposed to attending a nursery class in an out-of-borough special school.

A major benefit of a mainstream nursery is the opportunity for the visually impaired child to mix with fully sighted children. The wealth of experience available in a well-equipped, well-staffed nursery is immense. The language development of the visually impaired child may differ substantially from that of the fully sighted child so it is an advantage to be surrounded by the full range at the pre-school level. Chapman and Stone (1988:84) state that: 'The blind child misses out on a whole range of opportunities for self . . . initiated contingent exchanges and this is likely to have a generally delaying effect on language acquisition.' Many severely visually impaired children develop quite complex language structures at an early age, merely by 'parroting' what they hear with no understanding of meaning. This is one of the reasons why a high level of individual support is required at an early stage – to enhance the language the child is hearing and make it meaningful without using sighted language.

Although it is important for parents to have an overall view of what their locality has to offer in terms of nurseries and schools, time can be wasted looking at local provision only to discover that staff have never encountered a visually impaired child before, let alone a totally blind child. Parents can feel uncomfortable if staff unwittingly present a negative attitude owing to fear of the unknown, the extra workload envisaged, the lack of qualified staff, the presence of other children with special needs and the stress they are already feeling. While understanding such reactions, I feel the child should be viewed first and foremost as someone with the same needs as any other young person: a positive welcome, warmth, affection, praise and stimulation. The special requirements due to visual impairment are secondary to these basic needs.

Wentworth Nursery in Hackney has accommodated five visually impaired children over a number of years – two totally blind children and three partially sighted. Wentworth was originally chosen simply because it was a blind child's local nursery and the head was willing and interested in taking on the challenge. At the time this was a completely new experience for all the staff but it worked well and paved the way for future visually impaired children. While the premises might not be ideal, and the nursery has not been local to all the children, staff attitudes to special needs are far more important. During the discussion phase with parents a preliminary visit is arranged to meet the head and the staff and, if possible, to see the integration of a visually impaired child in practice. This is important as it is not always easy to imagine how it works. Parents who are anxious about their child's future are often reassured by what they see.

The Special Needs Assistant (SNA) currently supporting a blind child in the nursery has gained much useful experience of visually impaired children over the last 8 years; her confidence and expertise are encouraging for new parents.

The staff at Wentworth nursery are aware of the benefits of integration for the visually impaired child and feel that its success is dependent on the full-time support the child receives. Difficulties that can arise concerning the inclusion of a blind child are:

- How to adapt certain stories to make them meaningful?
- How much leeway to allow the blind child as regards behaviour that would be unacceptable from the other children, such as the enjoyable habit of 'swiping' equipment off the table and hearing it clatter on the floor?
- How much individual time should a nursery teacher give the visually impaired child who already has individual support?

These issues can be discussed as they arise or at an INSET session.

The educational psychologist and statementing process

The considerable amount of support available from the LEA, Social Services and Health Authority in Hackney has meant that no visually impaired child, to my knowledge, has needed a Statutory Assessment under the age of 2 years. The Children Act (1989) aims to ensure that parents receive information about the support available in their area for children 'in need'.

The Educational Psychologist is usually introduced because a Statutory

Assessment needs to be initiated. The stages recommended in the DFEE's *Code of Practice on the Identification and Assessment of Special Educational Needs* (1994) are not adhered to for a pre-school child. A blind child will obviously need individual support in the nursery setting, so a Statutory Assessment, resulting in the issuing of a Statement, is inevitable. A joint visit with the Educational Psychologist is arranged. The Educational Psychologist details the formalities of making a request for a Statutory Assessment to the Pre-Assessment Panel. We often make a joint presentation to ensure a full view of the child's needs. The Pre-Assessment Panel then decides, on the evidence submitted, whether or not a Statutory Assessment is necessary. When a totally blind child is involved reports are generally self-evident; a partially sighted child's needs may not be so clear cut and reasons for a Statutory Assessment may have to be indicated in more detail.

Once the Pre-Assessment Panel have agreed to a Statutory Assessment, reports are requested from the professionals listed in the Educational Psychologist's original report. My involvement at the stage of full assessment is generally that of submitting my own report and supporting the parent to some degree in completing hers. In Hackney there is a Parent in Partnership co-ordinator who can be contacted if more than minimal support is required by the parent.

When all the child's Statutory Assessment reports have gone to the Special Educational Needs Panel a draft Statement is generally produced and sent to parents. A copy is also sent to the Primary and Specialist Support Team (PSST) manager so that teacher support and/or SNA support can be arranged. Because of my involvement prior to the commencement of the statementing process I will already have alerted the PSST manager about the need for support in advance.

Child's introduction into nursery

Children admitted to nursery at the early age of two and a half years usually begin on a part-time basis. This might be a couple of mornings a week initially, the hours building up gradually over the first half-term. The parent is encouraged to stay for as long as the child seems to need her presence, perhaps leaving for short periods of time and then coming back, so that the child begins to learn that her departure does not mean she has gone forever. This can be a particularly difficult time for totally blind children. As far as the child is concerned once something or somebody cannot be heard or touched they have disappeared altogether. Only through experience can the child learn that this is not so. This must be done gently and sensitively if the child is to trust adults in the future.

The child with poor vision, or no vision at all, must rely completely on the honesty of others. It is extremely confusing to be told that a parent has gone to the shops, only to hear her voice in the background.

It is equally important for a parent not to threaten a child with leaving. During a child's first week in the nursery I have heard parents say that if the child does not behave and be 'good' they (the parent) will leave immediately. Such threats result from parents' anxiety for their child to fit into the regime. The reality is that it is fine for a child to take time to settle and to build up confidence slowly in new surroundings and with new adults; this cannot be rushed. Much will depend on whether or not the child has attended a playgroup or toddler group prior to entering the nursery; if they have, then separation may not be an issue. However, being in a new environment may still make the child feel insecure and trigger old feelings of the original separation.

The Code of Practice (page 103, paragraph 5:22) states that: 'LEAs should informally review a statement for a child under 5 at least every 6 months to ensure that provision is appropriate to the child's needs'. This is an excellent opportunity for all involved with the child to come together and share what is going well and any difficulties that may have arisen. The child's Individual Education Plan (IEP) can also be updated at this review with the setting of some realistic targets.

When the child actually starts in the nursery any questions from the other children should be answered with simple, but truthful, explanations. It is important to remember that the congenitally blind child may not know that he cannot see; seeing for him is using the sense of touch. He may still have to learn the fact that other people see in a different way. The reaction of others is therefore important to the visually impaired child's developing self-image. Any INSET sessions at the nursery would include planning for other children's reactions.

INSET (In-Service Training for Teachers)

It is vital to run an INSET session before the child starts at the nursery and very useful to have another after the child has settled. When staff have had some 'hands-on' experience with the visually impaired child, concerns and queries will inevitably arise. These are often dealt with during monitoring appointments, but can be discussed in more depth during a further INSET session.

Practical sessions, to gain an understanding of visual impairment, are vital, and far more likely to be remembered in a meaningful way. Theory is interesting and useful at times, but not necessarily helpful in the day-to-day working situation with the child.

The only real way to gain an understanding of how a blind child functions and makes sense of the world, is to blindfold oneself. Carrying out everyday tasks while attempting to follow instructions is not easy. It is surprising how visual our language is, and the real challenge is to make it as precise as possible, in a way which can be helpful to all children.

The best mock activities are those involving group participation where the visually impaired child is expected to join in with his sighted peers. Take for example a simple ball game: the teachers, playing the role of children, stand in a circle wearing blindfolds, and the person in the middle throws the ball to an unsuspecting 'child'. The game is played for a few minutes and then played with names being called out before the ball is thrown, so that each person is able to anticipate its arrival. Discussion about how this felt then follows – both initially when the ball came with no warning and secondly when people had been alerted. The difference that stating a child's name can make to the blind or severely visually impaired child is enormous. Because the nursery staff have experienced this for themselves they are more likely to remember the implications when lots of other individual needs are being catered for during the busy working day.

Monitoring and liaising

Regular visits are made to the nursery to discuss activities, suitable materials and equipment, the child's progress and any difficulties that have arisen. Sometimes the parent joins us at the nursery to contribute to the discussion. A common problem that causes concern is the child's insistence on poking or knuckling his eye, a blind mannerism which needs to be gently discouraged, usually by distraction with another activity.

Equipment and materials

The games and toys found in nurseries are generally suitable for visually impaired children without too much adaptation. The large outdoor pieces of apparatus are particularly appropriate; trolleys and prams are useful because the child can push them without worrying about coming to any harm as the trolley acts as a buffer and makes independent movement safer. Obviously the welfare of other children has to be taken into account and the child has to learn to move with care.

Construction toys and inset puzzles are suitable for visually impaired children. Other indoor games and table activities may pose problems at times, but most can be adapted with the use of different textures or the addition of some shaped or brailled clear plastic labelling foil (which is transparent and adhesive backed). Painting can be made into a tactile activity with the addition of glue, sawdust, broken up crisps or flour.

The totally blind child, who is inevitably going to need to learn braille eventually, will need a Perkins brailler in the nursery. As with any reading and writing readiness, there is a large amount of pre-braille work to be done. Until the child has built up a certain amount of finger strength, dexterity, and tactile discrimination, through other activities, the brailler is ineffective. However, the child may show some interest in the sound of the keys being pressed down and the bell that rings at the end of a line of braille. The SNA may use the brailler at times for notices around the room or writing the child's name to put on a picture or coat peg. By doing this she is modelling positively the blind child's form of communication. It is vital that everyone sees braille as something exciting and a medium to be respected in the same way as the printed word.

Small pieces of equipment are usually bought by the nursery but larger more expensive items such as a brailler are purchased by Hackney Education.

Conclusion

The Code of Practice (DFEE, 1994: p.15, para. 2:38) states that:

> Effective action on behalf of children with special educational needs will often depend upon close co-operation between schools, LEAs, the health services and the social services departments of local authorities. The Children Act 1989 and the Education Act 1993 place duties on these bodies to help each other.

Two years ago we formed a 'Vision Team' at the Donald Winnicott Centre, comprising the Educational Psychologist responsible for visually impaired children, rehabilitation workers from the Social Services Sensory Impairment Team and health workers at the Donald Winnicott Centre. We meet alternate months to discuss concerns about individual children and larger issues such as parental access to professionals. This has been extremely beneficial in the development of good communication practice. A register of visually impaired children has been created and is regularly updated. One of the main advantages of the existence of such a team is that children who are identified as having visual problems at a relatively late stage, for example between the ages of 5 and 11 years, can immediately be referred to all agencies as a priority. Children who enter the authority in the middle of their education can also be referred in the same way. Fewer children are likely to be lost in the system as a result. Liaison with health professionals and social services continues outside these arranged times.

The successful integration of a young visually impaired child depends on input from a variety of professionals and organisations prior to the child's admittance to school. Building up trusting relationships between both professionals and parents is vital so that everyone is working towards the same objective. This does not mean that there is never conflict or disagreement, but the existence of mutual respect helps to overcome many potential problems.

References

Chapman, E. K. and Stone, J. M. (1988) *Special Needs in Ordinary Schools, The Visually Handicapped Child in Your Classroom*. London: Cassell Educational.

Department for Education and Employment (1994) *Code of Practice on the Identification and Assessment of Special Educational Needs*. London: HMSO.

Department of Health and Social Security (1989) *The Children Act*. London: HMSO.

Jackson Education Service District (1978) *Oregon Project for Visually Impaired Children*. Medford, Oregon: Jackson Service Education District.

Suggested further reading

Bee, H. (1985) *The Developing Child*. London: Harper and Row.

Ellis, A. and Frankenberg, A. (1991) *What Shall We Do To Help? A Guide for Mainstream Nursery and Playgroup Leaders caring for Visually Impaired Children*. London: Royal National Institute for the Blind.

Gale, G. (1983) *What's this Blind Child Doing in My Class?* Melbourne: Royal Victorian Institute for the Blind.

Gregory, R. L. (1977) *Eye and Brain, The Psychology of Seeing*. London: Weidenfeld and Nicholson.

Royal National Institute for the Blind (1995) *Play It My Way*. London: HMSO.

Chapter 8

Supporting Deaf Children in the Early Years: An Inclusive Approach

Mary Robinson

Introduction

The history of deaf education in Britain in this century is one of increasing opportunity in terms of the recognition of individual rights to schooling and a much slower development of the right to choose how the deaf will gain access to information. Kyle and Woll (1985) explain this conflict in terms of the difference between educational aims of 'normalisation' and the deaf child's need to acquire access to information by the most efficient means available. This chapter describes the way in which one Local Education Authority, committed to inclusion for all children, organises support for the pre-school deaf. The approach is 'bilingual' and is based on the notion that deaf children and adults are a section of the population who make alternate use of two or more languages. Central to the provision of support for the pre-school group is the widely held belief that early intervention is essential (Riko *et al.*, 1985) and the policy emphasises the need for good quality involvement from the point of diagnosis, with a smooth transfer into formal education.

Current practice in the early years will be described in the context of some of the major issues in deaf education in general, and early provision in particular.

Identification of deaf children

Latest figures indicate that there are nearly 100,000 profoundly deaf adults in the United Kingdom, although the figure for adults experiencing some degree of hearing loss is closer to 3 million. 8,000 children in education at any time receive support for hearing and of these approximately 2,500 are diagnosed as profoundly or severely deaf. In the London Borough of Newham in the East End of London the number of children diagnosed as profoundly or severely deaf has risen steadily over the past 20 years and a recent estimate puts the figure of deaf children aged 0–19 years as 130. Of these, 29 are under 5 years of age and are supported in a variety of ways:

- 11 are supported at home by the pre-school service for deaf children.
- 6 attend a specially resourced nursery within a primary school.
- 4 have transferred into the reception class within the primary school.
- 5 attend other special or resourced schools within the borough.
- 3 attend schools outside the borough.

Generally diagnosis is occurring at an earlier age as improvements in technology and screening become more focused. Traditionally it was often parents (or grandparents) who first realised that there was a difficulty during the second year of life when the first words did not come. While that continues to be the case in some instances, the more usual picture is that of the child identified either through early testing owing to familial history or because of performance in the screening test in the latter part of the first year. As diagnosis occurs earlier, it is important that the support needed by families and children is co-ordinated so that the response can be both immediate and appropriate. Marschark (1993) talks of parents who participate in early intervention programmes as having 'the opportunity to begin a "remodelled" social relationship with their infant'. It is also crucial that parents are allowed to regain the confidence which the diagnosis may threaten.

In Newham, this early response was central to the development of policy and was based on the research being carried out in countries such as Sweden (Heiling,1995) and the USA (e.g Lederberg *et al.*, 1991) which focused on developing language in the first instance and treating the child as bilingual rather than impaired. Closer to home, observations and discussion of the 'Leeds Model', with the central role of British Sign Language (BSL) helped to facilitate the drafting of a model suited to the needs and diversity of the local population. As will be seen, this approach had a major impact on early support and the choices and options available to parents.

Developing a policy

By the end of the 1980s Local Education Authorities in Britain had acknowledged the need for a range of policies for educating all the children within their boundaries. For deaf children the policy adopted was often a restatement of what the local provision for the deaf had to offer. The differences were described in terms of the emphasis placed on oral and manual communication. The 'oral' approach focused on spoken language, the 'total communication' approach on oral language supported and reinforced by the use of signs or signed English, while the 'bilingual' approach recognised British Sign Language as the first language of the deaf. (For a detailed discussion of these approaches see Lynas, 1994.)

In the latter part of the 1980s, Newham had a provision for the deaf which had moved from the 'oralist' to the 'total communication' approach, with well-developed interagency liaison and early nursery provision. Children were supported at home initially and parents encouraged to ensure that hearing aids were worn. There was also an emphasis on the importance of play and stimulation, understanding behaviour and the importance of encouraging communication. Children entered nursery from about the age of two and a half and stayed there until 5 years of age. At that point they transferred to one of four places:

1. The Partially Hearing Unit (PHU) within the borough.
2. The local primary school with peripatetic support.
3. An outborough day school for the deaf which also followed a total communication approach.
4. A residential school for the deaf where the use of sign was the main method of imparting knowledge.

The decision as to which choice was made depended very much on the level of deafness of the child, the presence or otherwise of additional needs and parental views.

At that time Newham had adopted a policy of inclusion committed to educating children with special needs within the mainstream system. With increasing numbers of children with learning difficulties being educated in neighbourhood schools, it became important to explore the best method of meeting the needs of deaf children in the light of both equal opportunities and inclusion. In developing the policy, local councillors and education officers took into consideration the limited research information available here and in other countries, the approaches of other LEAs with a similar population and the need to ensure that what was provided for deaf children met the inclusive criteria of quality education, provided locally in the company of age-appropriate peers. Within this it was important to identify what support systems would be needed in order to foster successful learning. The policy adopted was that of 'bilingualism', with an emphasis on early identification, involvement of deaf adults, the development of British Sign Language as well as oral language and the delivery of the curriculum through both English and BSL. The implications of the adoption of this policy for the population of children under 5 centred on the nature of early support and the experience of a mainstream nursery.

Communication options

Any discussion about meeting the needs of the pre-school deaf brings into sharp relief the debate about how the deaf child develops communication. As the crucial importance of the 1–3 age range for the development of language has become established (Bruner, 1977), so both sides of the debate have focused on teaching the young child to communicate during this period. Since much of parent–child interaction is visual and physical in the first year (Hammar, 1980) and most children are diagnosed as deaf in the second year of life there are likely to be relatively few differences in the way deaf children are treated during their first year of life. Parents frequently report that they are made aware of a hearing difficulty in the child by their lack of responsiveness or their watchfulness. However, this often leads to a redoubling of effort on the part of the parent to try to elicit a response. It is often only when the expected words do not appear that parents seek help and by that time they will frequently have a range of worries which may or may not include deafness. It is what happens after diagnosis that causes theorists to disagree and the conflicting advice that abounds can be distressing to parents. In the oralist tradition the focus in these early years is the maintenance of spoken language with greater emphasis on shaping the response of the child. The use of hearing aids and the development of listening skills are paramount, as is the insistence that the child enters fully into the hearing world and has maximum exposure to language.

The bilingual approach sees the first year as setting the foundation for communication but also sees the failures which result sometimes in the child switching off or the parent becoming frustrated. The aim here is to introduce the parent to the world of the deaf through involvement with deaf adults and other deaf children and to focus on the child using vision and gesture as well as hearing to develop communication. This does not preclude the use of spoken language and there is a similar emphasis on use and maintenance of hearing aids, talking to and around the child and gaining as much response as possible. The only difference is that the focus shifts from gaining understanding through speech to gaining understanding by whatever means possible.

In assessing the communication development of young deaf children it is important to remember that many formal tests designed to determine the language competence of children do so through the medium of English. Even when they are delivered through sign, results may give only a very sketchy picture of the child's communication skills. In Newham assessment is based on the child's use and understanding of language, both sign and spoken, and the way in which these allow the child to gain access to information and to express their own ideas. Video recording is routinely used and it is hoped in the near future to refine these assessments so that the bilingual approach can be compared more directly with the other approaches available.

The bilingual approach is strongly pragmatic and it seems likely that the shift in focus to developing 'communicative competence' (Hynes, 1972) may provide an alternative to the choice between communication options and the need to defend a particular style or approach.

Supporting parents

Most areas provide some support to parents at the time when their child is diagnosed as deaf. A survey of Local Education Authorities, Health Authorities and Social Service Departments, carried out between March and June, 1993 (reported by Turner, 1994) looked at the way co-operative practices are being developed in the light of the 1989 Children Act and the setting up of Joint Registers of Children with Disabilities. While the pattern of provision varies, education frequently plays a lead role and there is widespread collaboration between LEA Services for Hearing Impaired Children and Health Agency Audiology Services. However, only 12.5% reported a joint register at the time of the survey.

In Newham there is a history of good inter-agency work with children under 5, co-ordinated through the Child Development Centre. Close links are maintained between the Paediatric Audiology department and the Service for Deaf and Partially Hearing Children. The shift in policy has maintained this link and allows for very early involvement with families of the deaf child. A teacher from the service will often be present at the time of diagnosis and can set up contact from that point. The role of the teacher here is to reinforce and explain information given at the time of diagnosis but not necessarily 'heard' by the parents. The knowledge that a child is deaf will be equally devastating for any parent or carer, but the awareness that there exists a framework of support and a planned approach to meeting communication and educational needs, to which they can have immediate access, may at least reassure them that theirs is not the only deaf child and that their child has a future.

In a practical sense the teacher of the deaf guides the parents through the next few months while they are coming to terms with the deafness. The order of events may differ in each case but the teacher will ensure that:

1. The type and level of deafness is explained to the parent and the implications of this kind of loss are explored and discussed.
2. Hearing aids are fitted and the parents supported in introducing them to the child and encouraging their use.
3. The family is visited by a deaf adult working for the service who talks about what it means to be deaf and the variety of communication methods available to the child.
4. They hear about sign language, see it in use and observe the deaf adult interact with their child.
5. They are offered the opportunity to learn the basics of BSL in their home and to meet other deaf adults and children.
6. They will meet the range of professionals likely to be involved with their child and be able to discuss aspects such as education and social development.
7. They receive regular visits, possibly in the first instance from a deaf instructor and/or another member of the Service for the Deaf and Partially Hearing. This support is generally weekly, and focuses on parents maintaining their previous efforts to communicate and developing confidence in themselves as the primary communicators for their child.

This aspect of developing confidence is the key to supporting parents at this early stage. All too often parents describe 'losing' their deaf child (as indeed do the parents of many children with special needs) to the 'professionals' as the number of people who have a 'stake' in the child suddenly proliferates. While it is difficult to avoid this completely if the child is to be fitted with aids as soon as possible and communication is to be encouraged, it is important that parents are not overwhelmed and that their knowledge of their child is recognised and developed. Bouvet (1990) compares the position of parents of a newly diagnosed deaf child with that of the 'intuitive' parent of 50 years ago, when scientific thinking held that it was 'dangerous' to indulge an infant. It was the recognition of the infant's capacity for interaction with the mother that allowed the exploration of new perspectives in language acquisition. Similarly, it is the recognition that it is the commonality of the language needs of all children that is the most reliable guide to communicating with the deaf infant. Thus as far as possible there is a key adult who supports and introduces others as the family is ready and the time seems appropriate, e.g. the educational psychologist may not need to be involved until the parents ask about schools.

Observing parental confidence develop highlights many of the inconsistencies in the debate about which form of communication is best. Whatever theorists or educators advise, in reality parents and children will use any means possible to communicate with each other. Their 'freedom' to do so in any way they can is central to the bilingual policy. The belief is that the resulting quality of the relationship and the security of the child will more than compensate for any perceived lack or 'purity' in the child's developing communication skills.

Early education

Deaf children and their families are introduced to the deaf playgroup as early as possible. The purpose of the playgroup is to meet other deaf children and adults, for children to experience play and interaction with other children (deaf and hearing) and for deaf adults to have the opportunity to liaise directly with the children and their families. It is here also that parents often meet the other professionals involved with their children for the first time and get the opportunity to hear issues discussed without, at first, direct reference to their child. The resourced nursery encourages parents to visit regularly, staying and playing with their child and others and allowing the child to become familiar with the nursery environment. By the time the child is 3 years old they will be accepted into the nursery on an assessment basis and will generally attend full time if that is the parent's wish. Occasionally, parents prefer part-time attendance, at least initially, and this can easily be accommodated.

The children remain in the nursery until they are 'rising fives' and ready to transfer to the reception class. During that time their assessment is ongoing and staff liaise closely with speech therapist, psychologist, teacher of the deaf and deaf communicator in tracking the child's development and exploring the arrangements that need to be made for the child to learn successfully. A formal assessment is carried out, usually during the final term in nursery, because of the need at present to fund the resources which deaf children require. It seems likely that in the future the only children who will require formal assessment will be those who are experiencing difficulty within the school environment (i.e in exactly the same way as the majority of children's needs are met).

The nursery is resourced with extra staff, including a teacher of the deaf, a deaf communicator, a deaf interpreter and extra nursery nurses. At any time one or other of these staff will be available to support the deaf child in gaining access to the activities and experiences and involving them in dialogue about the things they are doing. In this way they aim to fulfil the natural development of language, i.e. that which develops through 'doing' and the need to convey ideas, ask questions and comment upon their environment. Parents are welcomed in the nursery at any time and are encouraged to join in school-based BSL learning. Regular contact is also maintained through the home–school record book (an important contact as many of the children come to school by bus).

The emphasis is on providing full access to the range of nursery experiences, while having the opportunity to have small group work to enhance speech and listening skills, develop attention and focusing skills and gain an understanding of stories. All children in the nursery are encouraged to communicate through both speech and sign, and staff are continually surprised by the facility for sign learning in very young children who are not deaf.

At the time of transfer these children have had the advantage of 4-5 terms of nursery education, opportunities for group and whole-class learning as well as individual language-based teaching. Reception class teachers report that as a group the children are well ready to transfer and adapt easily and quickly to the increased structure of the infant classroom.

Case study – John

John is the second child in a family of three and was diagnosed as severely to profoundly deaf at the age of 11 months. He had failed a routine screening test at his GP clinic and further tests were carried out at the local Audiology Clinic and then confirmed at a regional clinic when his parents requested a second opinion. He was first fitted with hearing aids at the age of 1 year.

His parents had noted that he was not as responsive as his older brother and was not babbling but they had put this down to the fact that he appeared to be a generally quieter child, more clingy and less independent than his brother. There was no history of family deafness and no reason for his deafness has been discovered.

Shortly after diagnosis the family were visited at home by the peripatetic teacher for the deaf. Both parents were anxious to make up for lost time in terms of communication and ensured that John wore his aids as much as possible. They were keen to learn sign, and this was taught initially at home by a deaf communicator and later in classes in the local school.

John was an extremely shy child when he joined the nursery at the age of 3 years. For the first term he was silent and watchful, only smiling occasionally, usually when playing alone or as part of a small group with the deaf communicator. Gradually he became more confident and was able to build on his excellent visual skills by imitating signs when with the other deaf children. As he became more confident in these, he gradually introduced them to his play with other children and with other staff in the nursery. In advice for his Formal Assessment (at the age of 3 years, 7 months), the Speech Therapist described John as having good communication and pre-language skills, able to maintain eye contact and to imitate signed and spoken words. At the time of writing he has spent his first full term in reception class and his recent annual review noted his progress in all areas of the curriculum. His number, writing and pre-reading skills are all age appropriate and he is a confident and popular member of the class. His parents report that over the past year he has made increasing use of his hearing and he is eager to use his voice, showing delight when he uses the right word.

Summary

The recent survey carried out by Bloor (1993) of the communication approaches in all LEAs in England found that increasingly more than one approach is being offered: 30% of services claimed to offer or make available all three approaches and over 50% offered at least a combination of two. The London Borough of Newham has pursued a bilingual policy for the past 4 years and the first children identified in the new Service for Deaf and Partially Hearing Children have just transferred into primary school. The new service undoubtedly benefited from being able to build on existing good practice such as the provision for early years education. While there have been inevitable 'teething troubles' and the process of problem solving is continuous, first impressions are those of confident and informed parents, who have good levels of communication with their children. The majority of children develop BSL as their first language, with some English and/or the first language used in the parental home. The children are well prepared for the transfer to primary school, are confident in their use of sign and have positive social relationships within the classroom. It now remains for the more concrete evidence to be collected and the questions posed which for years have dominated the education of the deaf. These must include:

- the effectiveness of the bilingual approach in the early years
- the focus on the development of BSL as a first language
- the impact on the development of literacy skills
- the effect on the child's social and emotional development

These issues can probably be studied thoroughly only through longitudinal studies such as that of Heiling (1995). Through asking the questions, collecting relevant data and comparing outcomes with those achieved under different policies and approaches, the bilingual approach to education of the deaf can be evaluated. It is crucial that policy development remains dynamic, incorporating new advances in knowledge and technology while aiming to provide the best possible education for all deaf children.

References

Bloor, D. (1993) *A Survey of Communication Approaches used in Pre-school/Primary Provisions for Deaf Children in England.* Unpublished MSc Dissertation. Manchester: Centre for Audiology, Education of the Deaf and Speech Pathology, University of Manchester.

Bouvet, D. (1990) *The Path to Language.* Clevedon, Pa: Multilingual Matters Ltd.

Bruner, J.S. (1977) 'Early social interaction and language acquisition'. In: Schaffer, H.R. (ed.) *Studies in Mother – Infant Interaction. Proceedings of the Loch Lomond Symposium, September, 1975.* New York: Academic Press.

Hammar, A. (1980) *The Deaf Child and the Hearing Teacher: a Bilingual Situation.* Paper read at the International Congress of Education of the Deaf, held 4-8 August, Hamburg.

Heiling, K. (1995) *The Development of Deaf Children: Academic Achievement Levels and Social Processes.* Germany: Signum.

Hynes, D.M. (1972) 'On communication competence'. In Pride, J.B. and Holmes, J. (eds) *Sociolinguistics.* Harmondsworth: Penguin.

Jordan, L. and Goodey, C. (1996) *Human Rights and School Change – The Newham Story.* Bristol: Centre for Studies in Inclusive Education.

Kyle, J.G. and Woll, B. (1985) *Sign Language – The Study of Deaf People and their Language.* Cambridge: University Press.

Lederberg, A.R., Willis, M.G. and Frankel, K.H. (1991) *A Longitudinal Study of the Effects of Deafness on the Early Mother–Child Relationship.* Paper presented at the biennial meeting of the Society for Research in Child Development.

Lynas, W. (1994) *Communication – Options in the Education of Deaf Children.* London: Whurr Publications.

Marschark, M. (1993) *Psychological Development of Deaf Children.* New York: Oxford University Press.

Reed, M. (1984) *Educating Hearing Impaired Children.* Milton Keynes: Open University Press.

Riko, K., Hyde, M.L. and Albert, P.W. (1985) 'Hearing loss in early infancy: incidence, detection and assessment'. *Laryngoscope*, **95**, 137–45.

Turner, S. (1994) 'Collaboration in support for the under-fives.' *Journal of British Association of Teachers of the Deaf*, **18**(5), 154-62.

Chapter 9

Language Impairment in Pre-schoolers

Lesley Fleming and Sue Sheppard

In this chapter we outline the nature of language impairment in pre-school children. This will be explored in relation to identification, assessment and interventions.

Defining terms

Before defining what constitutes a language impairment it seems essential to have a clear idea about the nature and functions of language at a general level. Language can be defined as a formal, shared, symbolic system. It allows individuals to communicate about ideas, experiences and objects which do not actually have to be present at the time. The focus here is on pre-school children and it will be argued that at this level language is much less abstract. This is not to underestimate the skills and knowledge present in even the youngest of language users. Young children can be both competent and extremely novel in their use of language.

Communication is present at the earliest stages of interaction between an infant and carers, and related to an understanding between at least two individuals. Bancroft and Carr (1995:52) propose that language develops, 'as a more effective means of communication rather than the first means'. The motivation for learning and using language occurs when the child comes to realise that prelinguistic behaviours are not sufficient to make his or her precise intentions known to another person. Young children soon realise the power of language in manipulating the actions of those around them. There seems to be no predetermined pathway for teaching children to communicate with others. The early play found between infant and carer is now recognised as being based on a more reciprocal relationship than previously held (Stern, 1985; Trevarthen, 1979). Recent work in developmental psychology indicates that many prelinguistic skills are evident even before a child's first words. These are believed to provide the building blocks of language. Foster (1990:18) suggests that for language to come 'on line' there is the need for a 'complex synthesis of cognitive processing, sensory information and affective development'.

Relationship between prelinguistic and linguistic behaviour

Prelinguistic communication will be taken here to describe the 'child's earliest intentional behaviour' such as turntaking, imitation, initiation, 'burst-pause' sequences, observation skills and gesture. Adults are often found to attribute intent to the actions, sounds and gestures of the young infant even when no intention may be implicit. To be intentional the behaviour has to convey information to another person or indicate a shared understanding of an action or situation. Yoder and Warren (1993) review the studies in this area and propose that there is likely to be a causal link between prelinguistic and linguistic communication development. Children with advanced prelinguistic skills seem more able to utilise adult input. These skills enhance their overall communication and facilitate verbal skills (Locke, 1990). It will be argued later in this chapter that where there are difficulties in language development, interventions based on prelinguistic behaviours can be effective in facilitating progress.

Theories of language development

Linguists and psychologists have long debated the nature of language development. Social learning theory argues that language has to be learnt over time and that this progress takes place through imitation, reinforcement and the shaping of communicative acts. Nativists argue that this cannot explain the creative and novel language often found amongst young children. They propose that there is an innate rule-driven system present in the infant which ensures they can understand and respond to the language to which they are exposed. It is argued here that a social interactionist perspective is nearer the truth as it accepts the contribution of both innate and early skills, as well as recognising the role of the environment, particularly at a social interpersonal level. It also highlights the more active role of the child in the process of learning language skills which is contrary to the more passive picture portrayed by the earlier models.

What is a language impairment?

Language impairment suggests a weaker system than that generally found. It does not imply that communication cannot take place, but that the refinement of messages between individuals is in some ways less effective. The term is not precise as diversity is prevalent within any population and it can be difficult to decide when a child has a 'real' difficulty as opposed to a 'perceived' one. The popular conception is to consider developmental milestones. Parents and professionals alike are heard to refer to information about 'first words' and 'length of utterances'. Comparing a child's progress to these socially constructed 'norms' can prove to be a very negative measure and reinforce the notion of a medical 'deficit' model requiring some form of treatment. It seems more productive to consider a child's communicative behaviours as a whole, including language and to identify their relative strengths as well as areas where refinement seems to be an issue for focus. Foster (1990) suggests that although the course of language development has been largely mapped out there would appear to be much evidence for variation in both the rate and style with which the skills are acquired.

The literature tends to focus on a distinction between language which presents as delayed as opposed to disordered (Lees and Urwin, 1991). This distinction is perhaps more useful when referring to older children but it proves highly problematic for pre-schoolers as the wide spectrum of abilities found can blur the boundaries between the two. A delay suggests that language skills are developing along similar patterns to that generally found, but that the progress is at a slower pace. Delays may be present in respect of immature phonology (speech sounds), the production of expressive language (spoken words) and receptive elements (comprehension) or indeed any combination of the three key areas. A disorder suggests that development would appear to be uneven and atypical in nature. The child appears to take a different route from the constructed 'milestone model' referred to earlier. Disorder generates the use of labels, e.g. dyspraxia, semantic–pragmatic disorder. Parents may prefer this, as it gives a reason for the difficulty, hence allaying feelings of 'guilt' and 'anxiety' over the child's progress. The delay model conversely generates a 'catch up' philosophy.

The use of labels can assist in explaining and understanding a child's needs and may portray a 'special image' that is more comfortable for parents and professionals alike. Thorough research of proven, effective means of intervention can also help guide those supporting children, e.g. the use of the TEACCH programme (Watson, 1985) for children identified as having Autistic Spectrum Disorders. A 'label' is, however, no more than a starting point and every child is worthy of an individualised approach, regardless of the terminology used.

Incidence and prognosis

Research indicates a high prevalence of communication difficulties in pre-school children (Webster, 1988). He suggests that 5% of children enter school with such difficulties. Law (1992) reviews the persistence of language impairments and finds that a large number of pre-school children who have early difficulties with language do go on to have longer term problems. Bishop and Edmundson (1987) produce some complex findings outlining the ability to predict good outcome according to the nature of the difficulty. Persistence difficulties can however translate into other areas of development and so it is important to acknowledge that this group is at risk and to monitor their early educational attainments with care on school entry. The Code of Practice (DfE, 1994) offers a useful and effective model for this to take place.

Assessment of children with language impairment

Educational Psychologists (EPs) frequently experience pressure from educational and health professionals such as Speech and Language Therapists to clarify whether a child has a specific language difficulty, that is, they are experiencing difficulty solely in the area of language,or more global/general learning difficulties, i.e. delayed development across many developmental areas. Historically it has been common for EPs to use a psychometric intelligence test such as the Weschler Pre-school and Primary Scale of Intelligence (WPPSI) to enable this distinction to be made. This assessment tool has been published for psychologists to use with young children, to obtain an Intelligence Quotient (IQ) i.e. an estimate of cognitive ability. It contains 11 subtests which have been subdivided into two distinct scales through a process of factor analysis, the Verbal Scale and the Performance Scale. The Verbal Scale is considered to contain the sub tests which are verbally loaded to the greatest degree. That is, some subtests are more saturated in 'verbal ability' than others (Elliot and Tyler, 1987). The Performance Scale contains those subtests which have the lowest verbal loading.

It is generally assumed by education and health professionals alike, that if a child scores below the average range on the verbal scale but scores above or within the average or above average range of the performance (non-verbal) scale she or he is considered to have a specific language difficulty. In contrast to this if a child scores below the average range on both scales she or he is assumed to have more general/global learning difficulties, commonly termed 'moderate learning difficulty'. These very distinct 'diagnoses' often lead to very different types of provision being made by education authorities to meet the identified Special Educational Needs and can have a significant and élitist influence on the future expectations of progress. It follows, therefore, that some children will be excluded from the term 'specific language difficulty' and subsequently considered ineligible for certain types of specialist provision because of their lower IQ or because of lower attainments in other curriculum areas (Fredrickson and Reason, 1995), as well as language.

Is it necessary to obtain an Intelligence Quotient (IQ) in the process of identifying and defining 'specific language difficulty'? Historically there have been many arguments made against the use of psychometric IQ tests (Gillham, 1978). Pre-school children, especially those who have difficulty processing language, are disadvantaged in many ways by such an assessment procedure. Psychometric tests such as the WPPSI are often administered on a 'one-off' basis by an unfamiliar adult in a context which is unfamiliar to the child. This is due to EPs being accommodated in a quiet area away from the busy nursery or playgroup setting, in an attempt to provide a distraction free environment for testing. Alternatively, assessment may take place within a clinic setting. The psychologist's attempts to communicate with the child are restricted by the necessity to use the set published scripts which are contained in the test manuals. This leads to the psychologist being unable to tailor language to the linguistic strengths and needs of the child. This situation is worsened by the unfamiliar format of the test items which are largely context irrelevant. These factors are compounded by the fact that the performance of a pre-school child is not necessarily consistent from day to day or during different parts of the day. Children also vary in their willingness to demonstrate their knowledge.

Children who are experiencing difficulty in the area of language are further disadvantaged by this type of assessment technique. They tend to be less experienced in using language, that is, they possibly talk less and are talked to less, and therefore are less likely to have access to the type of information required particularly in the verbal subtests. They are also disadvantaged by the fact that neither the verbal nor the performance subtests call upon abilities that are purely verbal or non-verbal (Elliot and Tyler, 1987). The performance of pre-school children on this test may be further suppressed by the fact that many of the verbal and performance subtests have lengthy verbal instructions which can be difficult for pre-school children, especially those experiencing difficulty processing language, to understand. It can also be difficult for a child of pre-school age to sustain their interest and attention throughout the long administration time of the culturally biased psychometric test.

In the light of the above, the necessity and usefulness of measuring IQ during the process of identifying and defining 'specific language difficulty' should be questioned. It has been argued that EPs are more effectively employed as interventionists, aiming to bring about change (Gillham,1978). The information provided by psychometric assessment tools such as the WPPSI does not empower the EP to facilitate and bring about change. The information provided during such an assessment does not naturally lead to intervention; that is, it does not inform us about what the child needs to learn next and how this can be taught and achieved in their pre-school educational context.

What type of assessment would be more informative? Psychologists working in partnership with parents and carers can obtain a more accurate, and valid picture of a child's developmental strengths and needs. This information is best obtained by psychologists through the use of semi-structured interview, consultation, direct observation and participation in a child's usual play activities. This has the advantage of the child being with known adults in a familiar context and encompasses the guidance offered by the Code of Practice for the Identification and Assessment of Special Educational Needs (DfE, 1994).

Interventions and the rationale behind them

The initial starting point for any intervention has to be each individual child's needs. It would be wrong here to be too prescriptive about which type of programme is needed to support young children with language impairments. There is a need to be flexible with any approach implemented and to review and modify targets according to the child's progress and any new emerging needs. An outline will be given here of the nature of some of the approaches to be found in place. There are perhaps two distinct types of interventions:

- Structured language programmes.
- Naturalistic models of interventions.

Structured Language Programmes

This type of approach encompasses specific targets which have been identified during assessment and are worked on individually or in small groups. These types of interventions usually focus on the more structural aspects of language acquisition and may be used by a range of professionals, in collaboration with parents. The children may be in pre-school or nursery provision, special units or have pre-school home visiting teachers. These approaches tend to be behaviourally based to varying degrees.

One example is the Derbyshire Language Scheme (Knowles and Masidlover,1982). The scheme directs adults to set up a range of concrete play and early language work based on language skills generally found amongst children up to the age of four and a half. There is a central focus on the comprehension of language and the number of information carrying words a child can act on. The technical side of recording and assessing the children can be frustrating at times but the scheme does perceive the child as being as active learner and has scope for flexibility. The Living Language scheme (Locke, 1985) is designed to support children from a pre-school age who are failing to speak spontaneously. There is an increasing acknowledgement of the richness of the adult–child interactive contexts and a focus on building on the child's interests and day-to-day experiences. The programme is divided into three key phases, all based on 'normal' developmental patterns of language acquisition. These are the Pre-Language programme, the Starter programme (first words) and the Main programme (putting words together).

The Portage system which is well documented (White, 1997), is a service which is usually implemented in the home, guided by specially trained pre-school home visitors. A developmental checklist is completed, from which targets can be set, and language is one of the scales considered. Parents implement the targets, keep records and new teaching activities can be modelled by the teacher on visits.

The above programmes have been criticised as they focus predominantly on 'normal' development patterns. It has been argued already that many children with language impairment follow more uneven patterns of development and may also have broader needs across other areas of their development.

Farrell (1992) in a reassessment of behavioural approaches acknowledges that there are problems generated when trying to teach language through an objectives-based model. The aim in supporting and developing language: 'is for the child to express new and creative ideas from within and not to have to follow a pre-determined path, as provided in a behavioural programme'.

Naturalistic interventions

This moves us on to the more naturalistic and interactive approaches influenced by Vygotskyian principles. It is argued here that it is too narrow to look at language interventions in formal structural ways in isolation. There may be the need for some structured support as above, particularly if concerns are very specific and persistent in nature. Although language skills and communicative behaviours can be very different and develop at different rates there seems to be some difficulty in separating out interactive behaviours from either area. Those following the ideas of Vygotsky would see that the adult's role is to, 'arrange experiences' for each child within their 'zone of proximal development' to promote progress. What the child experiences first in an interpersonal way, will later be internalised into an intrapersonal representation.

Within this type of approach there is still a need to use a framework for identifying needs and measuring progress. Useful schedules for this are the Pre-Verbal Communication Schedule (Kiernan and Reid, 1987) and the Pragmatics Profile of Everyday Communication Skills in Children (Dewart and Summers, 1995). These profiles are based on structured interviews with those who spend significant time periods with the child, e.g. parents, carers, teachers. From these profiles it is possible to identify areas where the child needs to build strategies for communicating needs and developing their language skills. They can be complemented by observations of the children in naturalistic settings. There is some evidence to suggest that the parents of children with language impairments are less responsive and more critical than parents with normally developing children (Law, 1992). This is not to suggest that the parents are deliberately acting in these ways, rather that the children can be more difficult to tune into, which in turn leads to a distortion of the relationship and type of interaction. This is also likely to be the case with other key people in the child's day-to-day life. To improve the quality of the relationships adults need to develop an awareness of the following three strategies (adapted from Sheppard, 1996) that can be encompassed into a more naturalistic programme of support:

1. *Contingent imitation* – This is where the adult imitates the child's behaviour. Dawson and Lewy (1989) found that such imitation increased the child's attention towards the adult allowing for the input to be processed more effectively. Snow (1989) found that the child was also more likely to imitate the adult in such instances. Shared attention is promoted and there is a clearer reason for communicating through verbal or non-verbal means.

2. *Contingent responsiveness* – Goldberg (1977) suggests that responsiveness to a young child's communicative behaviour is facilitative of language and communication development for two reasons. It may enhance the child's belief that his or her acts can have an effect on the world and it may also shape more conventional communicative behaviour. The adult needs to become tuned into any spontaneous actions of the young child, such as sounds and non-verbal behaviours and use these to direct the interaction. By the adult suggesting the child has displayed intent and control, the child may come to take a more active role. A 'running commentary' approach from the adult is often a helpful strategy.

3. *Social routines* – Using repetitive and predictable turntaking games such as physical play, ball activities, action songs or table-top games, means that the child can concentrate on the actual interaction without the uncertainty of 'not knowing' what comes next. The use of a framework allows for experimentation on the child's part within a safe and secure context. Snow *et al.* (1987) found that these types of routines were powerful elicitors of communicative behaviour, both verbal and pre-linguistic.

Features of naturalistic interventions are that there is a highly child centred focus with less pre-established expectations than with the more structured schemes. Christie *et al.* (1992) argue that children with social and communication disorders require an extended period of 'active pre-verbal' dialogues built on the child's spontaneous actions and utterances. Sherborne developmental movement (Sherborne, 1990) is another intervention increasingly used to support pupils with communication difficulties. Evaluations to date are based predominantly on single-site case studies (Sheppard, 1994) but are suggestive of positive effects in respect of communicative behaviour. The child is seen as a reciprocal participant in such programmes as are the parents or carers and other supporting adults. Indeed these naturalistic models can fit into typical home-based activities, involving the whole family, as well as the pre-school provisions typically found. The aim is always to find as far as possible the optimal context for facilitating communication and increasing language use. The 'process of communication' is seen as the key as opposed to any product.

Conclusion

The nature of language impairment in pre-school children has been explored at levels relating to identification, assessment and interventions. It has been argued here that a balance of assessment techniques is required to inform practice. Assessment should be collaborative, involving those who are familiar with the child. Interventions based on contingent styles of support are advocated here as being amongst the most promising approaches for young children due to their naturalistic slant. Evidence remains inconclusive in this area and further research is vital. This will enable parents and practitioners to implement programmes secure in the knowledge that they are rooted in definitive and tenable research.

References

Bancroft, B. and Carr, R. (1995) *Influencing Children's Development*. Blackwell: Open University.

Bishop, D. and Edmundson, A (1987) 'Language impaired 4 year-olds: distinguishing transient from persistent impairment', *Journal of Speech and Hearing Disorders*, **52**, 156–73.

Christie, P., Newson, E., Newson, J. and Prevezer, W. (1992) 'An interactive approach to language and communication for non-speaking children'. In *Handbook of Child and Adolescent therapy in Britain*. Milton Keynes: Open University Press.

Dawson, G. and Lewy, A. (1989) *Autism: Nature, Diagnosis and Treatment*. New York: Guildford Press.

Dewart, H. and Summers, S. (1995) *The Pragmatics Profile of Everyday Communication Skills in Children* (Revised). Windsor: NFER Nelson.

DfE (1994) *Code of Practice on the Identification and Assessment of Special Educational Needs*. London: HMSO.

Elliott, C.D. and Tyler, S. (1987) 'Learning disabilities and the intelligence test results: A principal components analysis of the British Abilities Scales', *British Journal of Psychology*, **78**, 325–33.

Farrell, P. (1992) 'Behavioural teaching: A fact of life', *British Journal of Special Education*, **19**(4), 145–48.

Foster, S. (1990) *The Communicative Competence of Young Children*. London: Longman.

Frederickson, N. and Reason, R. (1995) 'Discrepancy definitions of specific learning difficulties', *Educational Psychology in Practice*, **10**(4), 195–207.

Gillham, W. (ed.) (1978) *Reconstructing Educational Psychology*. Beckenham: Croom Helm.

Goldberg, S. (1977) 'Social competence in infancy: a model of parent child interaction', *Merrill Palmer Quarterly*, **23**(3), 163–77 (as cited in Warren and Yoder, 1993).

Kiernan, C. and Reid, B. (1987) *Pre-verbal Communication Schedule*. Windsor: NFER Nelson.

Knowles, W. and Masidlover, M. (1982) *Derbyshire Language Scheme*. Derby: Derbyshire County Council.

Law, J. (1992) *The Early Identification of Language Impairment in Children*. London: Chapman and Hall.

Lees, J. and Urwin, S. (1991) *Children with Language Disorders*. London: Whurr Publishers.

Locke, A. (1985) *Living Language*. Windsor: NFER Nelson.

Locke, J. (1990) 'Babbling and early speech', *First Language*, **9**(6), 191–206.

Sheppard, S. (1994) *An Evaluation of Sherborne-based Developmental Movement: A Single-site Case Study Focusing on Pupils with Difficulties in Communication and Social Interaction*. Dissertation submitted in partial fulfilment of the requirements for the MSc in Educational Psychology, University of East London.

Sheppard, S. (1996) *The implementation of Sherborne-based developmental movement with pupils on the Autistic continuum*. Therapeutic Interventions in Autism. Conference proceedings – Durham, April 1996. National Autistic Society, Autism Research Unit (University of Sunderland).

Sherborne, V. (1990) *Developmental Movement for Children*. Cambridge: Cambridge University Press.

Snow, C.E. (1989) 'The uses of imitation'. In Speidal, G.E. and Nelson K. (eds) *The Many Faces of Imitation in Language Learning*. New York: Springer Verlag, pp.103–29. (Also cited in Yoder and Warren, 1993).

Snow, C.E., Perlmann, R. and Nathan, D.C. (1987) 'Why routines are different'. In Nelson, K. and Van Kleek, A. (eds) *Children's Language*, Vol 6. Hillsdale, N.J.: Lawrence Erlbaum Associates, pp.281–96.

Stern, D.N. (1985) *The Interpersonal World of the Infant*. New York: Basic Books.

Trevarthen, C. (1979) 'Communication and cooperation in early infancy: A description of primary intersubjectivity'. In Bullowa, M. (ed). *Before Speech*. Cambridge: Cambridge University Press, pp.321–47.

Watson, L.R. (1985) In Schopler, E. and Mesibov, G. (eds) *Communication Problems in Autism*. New York: Plenum Press, pp.187–206.

Webster, A. (1988) 'The prevalence of speech and language difficulties in childhood: some brief research notes', *Child Language Teaching and Therapy*, 4(1), 85.

White, M. (1997) 'A review of the influence and effects of Portage'. In Wolfendale, S. (ed.) *Working with Parents of SEN Children after the Code of Practice*. London: David Fulton Publishers.

Yoder, P.J. and Warren, S.F. (1993) 'Can developmentally delayed children's language be enhanced through prelinguistic intervention?' In Kaiser, A. and Gray, D. (eds) *Research Foundations for Intervention*. Vol. 2, *Enhancing Children's Communication*. Maryland: Paul Brookes Publishing Co., pp.35–61.

Chapter 10

Provision for Special Educational Needs in the Early Years: Policy and Procedures within one LEA

Janine Wooster and Ann Warn

Introduction

This chapter presents an overview of Kent's policy and procedures for Special Educational Needs in the early years with particular reference to the systems in North-West Kent. Specific references are made to the Code of Practice. We plan to concentrate on the role of the Early Years Assessment Manager (EYA Manager), take the reader through a step-by-step guide to Kent's local decision-making process and identify the local provision availability. The procedures will be illustrated first hand by case studies of two pupils progressing through the system.

Referral and assessment

Children are referred by a wide range of people including their own parents, Portage workers, occupational therapists, physiotherapists, speech and language therapists, paediatricians, social workers and play groups to the Early Years Assessment Manager for advice and support on placement and or interventions. The Early Years Assessment Manager will visit the family to observe and assess the child as shown in Figure 10.1. There is then the possibility of referring the child through a number of panels for consideration. If the child is already attending or is on the waiting list for a school nursery, then discussion can be held at the In-School Review with relevant professionals in attendance. The majority of pupils however would be discussed by the Pre-School Review Group with the involvement of the community paediatricians, physiotherapists, speech and language therapists, etc. The Pre-School Review Group can together look at the options available for the child and may suggest attendance at a pre-school group or visits from the Portage Service. The range of possible interventions is listed later in this chapter. The Pre-School Review may recommend that the child requires a statutory assessment of need according to the 1996 Education Act.

In this case information relating to the child will be passed to the Local Advisory Team – a group consisting of the Senior Officer in the Special Needs Section, an educational psychologist, a Special Educational Needs officer and a representative headteacher. All of the collated information will be considered in detail by the group and a decision will be made as to whether or not to begin a statutory assessment for the pupil. If not, the child will enter school in the normal way with recommendations for the appropriate support to be provided. If the decision is positive, reports are collected from all the relevant agencies and presented along with a proposed Statement of Special Educational Need to the Provision Advisory Team, within the 6-month deadline set by the *Code of Practice*. The Provision Advisory Team consists of the Special Educational Services Manager, the Assistant County Educational Psychologist, a special educational needs officer and a representative headteacher. All of the reports are considered and a decision is taken as to whether a Statement of special educational need should be issued, whether the wording is correct and what kind of provision needs to be made to meet the pupil's needs.

Keeping this model of the process in mind, we now elaborate on the role of the Early Years Assessment (EYA) Manager and outline the provision available to families at particular points in the system. Towards the end of the chapter, two case studies will be used to give an illustration of how the process works in practice.

Specific role of the Early Years Assessment Manager

The post of EYA Manager in North-West Kent is unique and was created in response to the 1989 Children Act. It is jointly funded, 50% by Education and 50% by Social Services Departments. In the other five areas of Kent, a pre-school adviser is in post, funded wholly by the Education Department. As the EYA Manager post was developed out of the pre-school adviser role, an additional .5 teaching time was provided to help to cover the case load of approximately 350 children in the Dartford, Swanley and Gravesham areas.

The main areas of responsibility are:

1. To visit and liaise with the various establishments – i.e. nursery classes, playgroups, family centres, health authority centres and

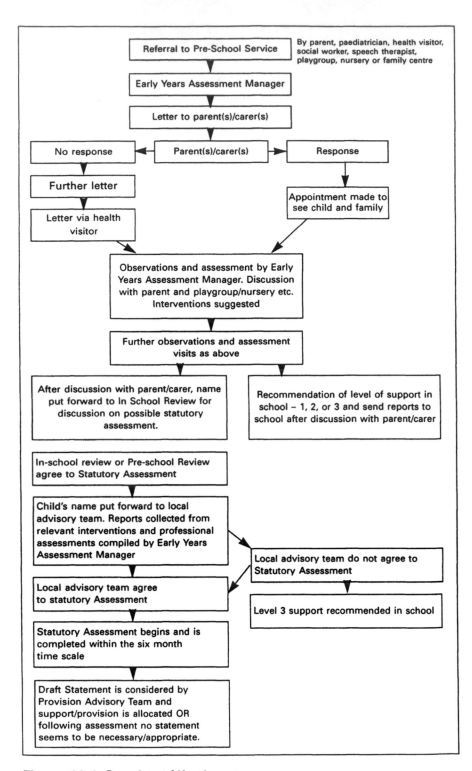

Figure 10.1 Overview of Kent's system

Portage, together with schools and voluntary services, and to offer advice on management and support for pupils with special educational needs.

2. To evaluate resources for pre-school children within the area and make recommendations for change and development (including reporting on playgroup provision in accordance with Section 19 of the Children Act).

3. To visit the parents of pre-school aged children with special educational needs, to counsel and advise the parents about issues relating to their child and to operate a standard recording procedure for visits to be updated and held at the Area Education Office.

4. To understand fully the criteria for statutory assessment and to be aware of the implications of such procedures for children under the Code of Practice.

5. To identify and assess pre-school children who have special educational needs within the terms of the 1993 Education Act; to offer appropriate advice relating to the completion of assessments and provision of statements and to compile Appendix D (educational advice) if required.

6. To liaise and co-operate with members of the local educational psychology service team.

7. To liaise as necessary with officers of the Social Services Department, Health Authority Trusts and voluntary groups.

8 To provide advice and assistance to the Area Special Educational Services Manager in prioritising the cases of pre-school children with special educational needs.

The EYA Manager also has 20 hours of secretarial time which is vital to the organisation and implementation of the process, systems and case work.

Table 10.1 indicates the kinds of provisions for ongoing assessment available for pupils when they have been seen by the EYA Manager. Pupils will enter at various points in the map of provision and some will move from one kind of provision to another, before entry to school.

Appendix 1 (see pages 122–4) illustrates the information collected and collated by the EYA Manager when attempting to determine the most appropriate provision. To enable pupils to begin school at five years or rising five, the Kent Audit Scheme enables the EYA Manager to complete the pre-school profile and suggest to a school that support is allocated within the levels indicated by the Kent Audit Scheme. The way in which the audit levels relate to the *Code of Practice* stages can be seen in Table 10.2.

	Age (years)	Provision accessed	
	0	Home visits by EYA Manager, teachers of the visually and hearing impaired – some respite care (provided by Health and Social Services Departments)	
	2½	Three assessment nurseries with some therapeutic input for children with a variety of special educational needs	Family Centre
Identification, assessment, advice and support from the EYA Manager	3	Pre-school Centre (Social Services HIghscope model). Playgroups (with special needs assistants if required). Education nursery classes. Assessment places in mainstream nursery school. Private nursery provision/day nurseries/child minders	Opportunity groups

Access to advice and intervention from therapists |
| | 4+ | Class in mainstream school for children with needs in autistic or social communica-spectrums. Designated schools for visually impaired, learning impaired or physically disabled pupils. | Family Centre

Opportunity groups |
| | 5 | Mainstream school with Levels 1, 2, or 3 support. Mainstream school with Statemented support and language unit. School for children with moderate learning difficulties School for children with severe learning difficulties. | Access to advice and intervention from therapists |
| | 8 | | |

Table 10.1 Provision in North-West Kent available from birth until school entry

Code of Practice stage	Kent audit levels
One	Level 1 – Provision to be given by the class teacher, in discussion with the school's SENCO.
Two	Level 2 – Partnership with other agencies needed. Support to be given by class teacher and SENCO, plus delegated hours from the Individual Pupil Support Service in the guise of Learning Support Assistants and specialist teachers.
Three	Level 3 – Partnership with agencies outside the school required – increased support from the Individual Pupil Support Service, Learning Support Assistants and specialist teachers, with advice from the educational psychologists, and possibly health and social services professionals.

Table 10.2 Relationship between Kent audit levels and the *Code of Practice*

If a pupil's needs are audited higher than Level Three, the support will be in line with the Statutory Assessment Process.

In order to inform the Area Special Educational Services Manager and the Regional Customer Services Manager about possible provisions that may need to be developed, the EYA Manager has devised a database. This not only records the progress of each child through the system, but also gives information about the specific needs of pupils and the type and quality of provision that will be needed in the future. This information is used by the SEN Team to assess the need for provision and it informs the purchasing of places within specialist provisions.

The use of all the available routes, the advice, support and intervention of the EYA Manager, the database and the local decision-making process ensures that the child will be matched to the most appropriate provision. Information collected by the EYA Manager is presented to a pre-school review meeting and subsequently passed on to the relevant people. All information is prepared in discussion with parents or carers and a standard identification/assessment format is used by the Pre-School Service (see pages 122–4).

The Code of Practice acknowledges the importance of partnership between the education, child health and social services staff. It is only through all these agencies working together that the special educational needs of children in the early years can be met. Parents or carers of children aged under 5 with special educational needs are encouraged to express a preference for provision which, resources permitting, is accessible through the local Special Educational Needs Department. In order to illustrate the progression of children through the system, the following case studies are presented.

Child A

Initially seen at the age of 2 years 11 months at a Family Centre (June 1995), where he presented with delayed expressive language, delayed fine motor control, short attention span, poor listening skills and emotional outbursts – advice was given on language activities and behaviour management.

He was seen again at a Highscope (Titchener and Titchener, 1991) pre-school centre run by Social Services at age 3 years 2 months (September 1995) and subsequently in October 1995, March 1996 and May 1996, where joint planning with staff at pre-school and from social services and health including the Speech and Language Therapist took place. Taking into account the quality and quantity of interventions which had occurred prior to school entry and his continuing delay with expressive language/listening skills and emotional outbursts, it was recommended that he should receive Level Three support on entry to mainstream school reception class as a rising five. He is due to start school formally in September 1996 and it has been recommended that he be reviewed at the first in-school Review to assess the appropriateness of the support offered.

Child B

Was referred to the EYA Manager after a developmental assessment at the age of 2 years 4 months (June 1994) and presented with delayed development and significant delay in speech and language. Contact was made by letter and subsequently telephone call to parents (July 1994). A visit was arranged for Autumn 1994 (2 years 10 months) to see him at his day nursery – advice and support was given directly by the EYA Manager and also through the support of a special needs assistant for two sessions per week. At the age of 3 years 4 months, he was again visited at the day nursery where the EYA Manager further discussed the possibility of Statutory Assessment with his parents. His case was presented to the Pre-School Panel (September 1995) and he was seen again (October 1995) to compile a report for the Local Advisory Team recommending statutory assessment. The Local Advisory Team approved the assessment to start in January 1996. The EYA Manager completed the educational advice (March 1996). The proposed Statement was written and considered by the Provision Advisory Team which agreed that the Statement be issued and a decision was taken that Child B should enter mainstream school with 10 hours from a learning support assistant in the classroom each week, plus outreach support from the Language Unit. It was recommended that the support be reviewed at the next in-school review.

Cases that have been presented were referred to the local authority at an optimum early stage. The system is developed in such a way that children can be slotted in at any age or stage. However, the later pupils are identified or referred, the more difficult it is to ensure intervention at the early stages and accurate assessment of their needs for appropriate targeted provision at school age. The in-school review system affords the opportunity to assess progress in mainstream schools or classes and to ensure that the support provided is targeted and appropriate.

In North-West Kent, schools forward their Reception class admissions lists to the Early Years Service. The Service in turn provides a written report (with parental consent) on interventions and levels of support required on entry into school. It may be that this service will eventually be available throughout Kent as headteachers find it very helpful in planning effectively for the children's school entry.

Future developments

> It is now broadly accepted that in the Early Years in particular, children's needs have to be seen as a whole . . . We should not underestimate the difficulty of co-ordinating our approach but in the interests of providing children with continuity and coherence and making the most efficient use of scarce resources then a co-ordinated policy with mechanisms for joint planning management and review must surely be a first priority.
>
> (Pugh, 1996:11)

Whilst North-West Kent has gone some way towards providing an integrated service there are still many posts and provisions that could be delivered in a more imaginative and integrated way. A service funded by Education, Social Services and Health Departments would be the optimum, particularly in the early years when each service works so closely with the family that it is, in effect, intertwined with all of the others. Each element of the service should be able to draw on the talents and experience provided in the others. Only then will children with Special Educational Needs and their families be offered a coherent and professional service capable of meeting those needs.

With this in mind, funding has been provided by the County for the initial stages of a response team to be in place by September 1996. There are also plans in two areas of the county to employ Early Years behaviour support staff.

Appendix 1: Early Years Assessment Service, Kent County Council. Pre-school profile: Identification and Assessment Form

Name:
Address:

Date of birth:
Receiving school:
Date of admission:
Recommended level of support:

Current pre-school provision:

Date of initial referral to pre-school:
By:
Referring problems:
Other agencies involved:

1. Self-help skills
   Toileting:
   Dressing:
   Feeding:
   Comments:

2. Physical development and health
   Health:
   Walking:
   Running:
   Climbing:
   Comments:

3. Language/communication
   Understanding:
   Speaking:
   Comments:

4. Play and social skills
   Solitary:
   Co-operative:
   Imaginative:
   Taking turns:
   Comments:

5 Cognitive abilities
  Puzzles:
  Attention to adult-selected activities:
  Colours:
  Matching:
  Sequencing:
  Concentration on own choice task:
  Comments:

6. Behaviour
  Response to instructions:
  Response to 'no':
  Comments:

7. Pre-reading/pre-writing skills
  Drawing:
  Looking at books:
  Tracing:
  Scissors:
  Comments:

8. Pre-numeracy skills
  Counting:
  Quantities:
  Shapes – Naming
          Matching
          Sorting
  Comments:

9. Additional comments/information

  Completed by:

  Signature:
  Name:
  Position:
  Date:

Observation sheet

Name:
Date of birth:
Chronological age:
Playgroup/nursery:
Supervisor/teacher:

Name	Action	Speech	Activity

Playgroup/nursery/family centre staff – comments:

Parental views/comments/information share:

Action:

By whom:

References

Pugh, G. (ed.) (1996) *Contemporary Issues in the Early Years* (2nd edn.) London: Paul Chapman.

Titchener, L. and Titchener, S. (1991) 'Form or content', *Special Children*, **49**, 21–25.

White, M. (1997) 'A review of the influence and effects of Portage'. In Wolfendale, S. (ed.) *Working with Parents of Children with SEN after the Code of Practice*. London: David Fulton Publishers.

Chapter 11

Principles into Practice: An Assessment Framework for Educational Psychologists

Fiona Barnett, Loraine Hancock, Julia Hardy and Marianne McCarthy

Context

The authors of this chapter work for Hammersmith and Fulham LEA. This is a inner-city borough with areas of economic disadvantage and a large under-5 population. The Psychology in Education Service places great emphasis on the early identification of special educational needs. Educational psychologists offer regular visits to nursery schools. Children who are under 5 and not in educational provision are allocated to an educational psychologist through a central register.

This chapter will describe the work that educational psychologists undertake when working with children who are under 5. Their work is influenced by the assessment framework that the Psychology in Education Service has developed as well as by the principles of good practice that are described in the Start Right Report (Ball, 1994). This report reviewed the nature of good early years practice and concluded that there are twelve principles which are fundamental:

1. Early childhood is the foundation on which children build the rest of their lives but it is not just a preparation for adolescence and adulthood; it has an importance in itself.

2. Children develop at different rates and in different ways – emotionally, intellectually, morally, socially, physically and spiritually. All are important, each is interwoven with others.

3. All children have abilities which can (and should) be identified and promoted.

4. Young children learn from everything that happens to them and around them.

5. Children learn most efficiently through actions, rather than instructions.

6. Children learn best when they are actively involved and interested.

7. Children who feel confident in themselves and their own ability have a head start to learning.

8. Children need time and space to produce work of quality and depth.

9. What children can do is the starting point in their learning.

10. Play and conversation are the main ways by which young children learn about themselves, other people and the world around them.

11. Children who are encouraged to think for themselves are more likely to act independently.

12. The relationships which children make with other children and with adults are of central importance to their development.

Assessment framework and the five dimensions of learning

The principles above acknowledge that the needs of young children are complex and interrelated. Therefore the assessment framework used by educational psychologists must demonstrate the richness of a child's development and ensure all facets are given due consideration. The assessment framework that has been developed by the Hammersmith and Fulham Psychology in Education Service aims to do this. This approach to assessment was developed to allow children the best opportunities to show what they can do in a familiar and supportive environment. This assessment framework is based on the work that is described by Barrs *et al.* (1990:6), 'The model has five parts, each of which is a different dimension of learning'. When we assess children's learning and development we need to understand what we observe. The five dimensions of learning develops a profile of a child's strengths and needs as a learner. The dimensions are interrelated and support each other:

1. Confidence, independence and interests.

2. Experience.

3. Knowledge, skills and understanding.

4. Strategies.

5. Reflectiveness.

There are a range of psychological theories and conceptual frameworks that underpin these five dimensions and guide us in our assessment and intervention work with the under-fives:

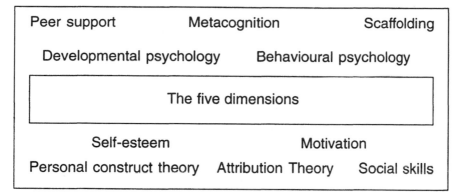

All five dimensions form part of a child's life as a learner. All assessment is context specific; it arises from and is affected by the learning opportunities that are offered and the social context in which it takes place. There is no such thing as a standard of competence which a child possesses independently of the circumstances in which he or she is developing. The dimensions of learning framework, as described by Boxer *et al.* (1991), offers a means of collecting evidence about a child in terms of his or her all-round development within the context of the nursery, home and wider environment. It offers a richer and more meaningful approach to assessment than the mere statement of a child's attainments, and it can offer insight and provide valuable information on which decisions about interventions can be made.

Assessments are based on information about a child's progress that is collected over time. A wide variety of sources of information are used, including systematic observations of the child in the normal learning context. All steps are taken to ensure that assessment techniques do not unfairly disadvantage specific groups of children. Careful consideration is given to the assessment of bilingual children. Assessments then lead to an agreed course of action which can subsequently be reviewed and evaluated. This is then clearly reported back to parents and other professional staff.

Dimensions of learning with practical illustrations from casework

What follows are examples of some of the psychological theories that underpin our work as well as some examples of our casework. Obviously all dimensions of learning are considered in our assessment and interwoven; however for the sake of clarity we will highlight each dimension separately to demonstrate how the framework supports our work.

Confidence, independence and interests

This dimension investigates a child's developing confidence, independence and interest as a learner and reflects a growing pleasure and involvement in learning. Any assessment makes judgements about a child's feelings and attitudes towards herself or himself. There are several psychological theories that influence this dimension, such as motivation, the wide area of developmental psychology and self-esteem. Self-esteem is an issue central to a child's development and can have either a positive or negative affect on this development. Children develop a positive self-esteem if they experience respect, are listened to and are cared for in a supportive environment. Children with poor self-esteem have low levels of confidence and may become isolated or have poor social skills when interacting with others.

Adam is a 3-year-old in a nursery who was referred to the Psychology in Education Service owing to speech and language difficulties as well as a lack of sustained play. He also demonstrated limited areas of interest in play and poor co-operative skills. The educational psychologist assessed this dimension through:

- observation in the nursery context;
- discussion with his mother and key worker;
- involvement in play in the nursery with a range of play activities such as puzzles, drawing etc.;
- discussion with Adam;
- observation of his response to a range of toys and activities.

The educational psychologist developed an intervention with the nursery staff and Adam's mother. One focus of this intervention was to build on Adam's interests and to extend his motivation to become engaged with a wider selection of toys and equipment. To do this the nursery looked at issues related to the grouping of children and peer support. Each day a member of staff spent 10 minutes engaging Adam with activities alongside other children. The adult gradually moved away to allow the group to play independently for increasing amounts of time. During this session new toys and activities were introduced and the adult modelled how the equipment could be used.

The nursery and Adam's mother felt there was a positive outcome to this intervention. Adam had made progress in all areas of his development; his language skills had developed and he had become more interested and focused in a range of equipment in the nursery. He also was spending more time interacting and co-operating with other children.

This dimension helped us focus on Adam's own interests and dispositions and how these were gradually extended to include playing with other children and adults. The importance of the adult's role is related to Vygotsky's notion of mediated learning and the importance of learning in a social context. The peer group was essential to the intervention.

Experiences

This dimension relates to a child's growing experiences as a learner and the range and variety of that experience. There has been a movement away from developmental theorists such as Piaget, who took a considerably child-focused view, with the child constructing progressively more powerful, abstract and integrated systems of knowledge by discovering how his or her actions affect reality, to a view that places more emphasis on the providers of experience. Vygotsky and Bruner move us further in focusing on the capacity to learn through instruction, work about the 'zone of proximal development' and how adults extend a child's learning through 'scaffolding'. This is demonstrated in our educational psychologist practice by focusing on 'why' questions as well as 'what' questions and investigating adult–child interactions. The practical example, which is discussed later, demonstrates Wood's idea 'that interactions between adults and children in "spontaneous" and 'contrived' encounters are different in nature' (1991:99). When Wood referred to 'contrived' he meant 'teaching/learning/testing encounters that are deliberately brought about by those in power (e.g. teachers or psychologists) as opposed to those which "arise" spontaneously out of child/adult contacts' (1991:99). It was assumed that interactions at home are more likely to be spontaneous and initiated by the child while those in school are usually contrived and adult centred. Wood suggested that the 'interactions follow different "ground rules" and create different demands of both the adult and the child' and that this is why children 'often appear to display varying levels of cognitive and linguistic competence in different situations' (1991:99).

Tizard and Hughes (1984:258) also concluded that 'judgements on children's language abilities should be very tentative until a context is found where they talk freely and spontaneously.' Several researchers, including Donaldson (1978), have demonstrated that young children often are able to do some things in some contexts but not in others. They have skills that do not always appear in their performance.

Wood and Wood (1983) worked with play-group leaders and nursery teachers. They found that adults who asked children many questions were less likely to receive questions from children, less likely to promote elaborated answers from children and less likely to encourage children to contribute spontaneously to dialogue. If children are questioned a lot, they show less initiative in their response. Also many of the questions that adults asked were of the closed variety. Being aware of this research suggests that, when working with young children, educational psychologists need to ask children better and fewer questions.

One way in which these theoretical perspectives have influenced practice is demonstrated in an assessment of 'John', an autistic boy. When the educational psychologist first became involved, the nursery talked about how 'unrealistic' his mother's expectations were of John. The educational psychologist observed John at the nursery and noted in her report that: 'At the nursery the educational psychologist did not hear John use much speech. He occasionally initiated contact with his key worker, but this was usually through gesture and sounds' and 'At the nursery, instructions frequently needed to be repeated before John would respond'. During a home visit the educational psychologist was very much struck by the different response and language that John was using. He talked to his mother using short sentences and responded to a range of suggestions on what he could do. Following these contrasting observations the educational psychologist returned to the nursery and discussed John's differing behaviour in the two contexts, suggesting ways of increasing John's speech and language in the nursery setting by altering the interactional style of staff.

Knowledge, skills and understanding

This dimension investigates both unconscious and tacit knowledge. When we think about this area of a child's development we use a variety of psychological theories such as the developmental theories of Piaget, Vygotsky, Bruner and their 'followers'; the behavioural theories which include the 'Learning Hierarchy', described by Haring *et al.* (1978) and approaches such as Portage; metacognition theories about children's awareness of their own learning and use of language. These theories influence the way information about this dimension is gathered about young children, for example through the use of checklists, observations, play sessions with the child and discussions with parents or carers and nursery staff. This information is best collected over time and in a range of settings. Two types of observations are frequently used: 'target child observation schedule' and 'participant observations'.

Target child observation schedule
This was developed by Sylva *et al.* (1980). During the observation the observer records what the child is doing in terms of activity, the language used and the social setting. This information is later coded. Analysing this data leads to investigating the amount of complex play the child was involved in as well the type of social interaction, such as parallel play or playing alone.

Participant observation

This is where the educational psychologist works alongside a child in the usual structure of the nursery setting and looks at the skills, language and understanding that the child demonstrates. Effective observation is dynamic and participant observation can identify what the child's next steps might be in relation to a particular activity. Observations reveal learning potential as well as what has already been achieved. Vygotsky's arguments show how 'learning which is orientated towards developmental levels that have already been reached is ineffective from the view point of a child's overall development. It does not aim for a new stage of the developmental process but rather lags behind the process' (1978:89).

One of the aims of early years education is to provide an environment where children can develop as autonomous, self-disciplined learners. Therefore assessment procedures need to reflect this aim. Educational psychologists frequently use what Wood (1991) describes as 'contingent teaching' when playing alongside young children; this is where a child is taught a new task, based on his or her previous interests and experience. The new task is taught through verbal prompting and demonstration. The child gradually begins to understand what is being said. An educational psychologist used this approach when working with Eve, a 3-year-old with Down's syndrome in a home setting. Using Makaton signing, Eve was able to copy 1, 2, 3. Eve's mother wanted her to build on this and develop an understanding of the conservation of number. Using practical activities relevant to Eve's age and skills, the educational psychologist demonstrated through contingent teaching how to support Eve to develop her skills of one-to-one correspondence when counting sets of one or two objects. This learning was also monitored with the aid of the 'Learning hierarchy' which identifies five stages in children's learning: acquisition, fluency, maintenance, generalisation and adaptation. Initially Eve was taught how to use a skill, then given practice so that she became fluent before she was shown how to generalise her knowledge to the nursery setting.

Strategies

This dimension deals with the learning and social strategies that children develop, often revealing a great deal about their views of the task, as well as their perceptions of social relationships. There is a wealth of theory and research in this area, both psychological and educational, such as peer support, metacognition, social skills and attention skills. Vygotsky believed that interactions between children are beneficial when a child is helped by another child who understands more about the activity. The more knowledgeable child may also benefit, as a result of explaining her or his ideas. Research by Glachan and Light (1982) supports this view: they explain that the results of various experiments show that children working together are able, in some circumstances, to solve problems and give explanations that they have not been able to solve or explain individually.

How many of us in our practical day-to-day advice suggest the use of peer support and possibly not all of us are aware of the research behind this! Much of the work of educational psychologists relates to children and adult strategies. In assessments we would pose a number of questions, such as:

- Has the child a range of strategies?
- Is he or she able to use them flexibly?
- Does he or she use some negative strategies?
- Do the strategies he or she uses reveal anything about the child's view of the activity?

We must also not forget to look at the strategies that children use in their relationships with peers. The theme of friendship impinges on the strategies dimension.

One child, Ayesha, aged three and a half who has only three words shows very little interest in constructive or imaginative play. After a number of observations of Ayesha at home and in the nursery the educational psychologist raised the issue of how Ayesha uses crying to communicate. For instance, once when sitting by a computer touch-screen she cried whenever the picture went blank but soon she learnt the effect of tapping the screen. However later that morning she became particularly upset when she touched the screen just with her fingertips and the picture did not come back. The educational psychologist worked with the staff to build upon Ayesha's interest in screens so this became part of her routine. Similarly Ayesha's mother observed that Ayesha seemed to need routine: one example was how Ayesha would cry if something different from the usual occurred (such as driving a different route). So the educational psychologist and parent together set up a programme in which photographs were used to indicate 'where next', which proved useful at times of changed routine.

Reflectiveness

This dimension relates to a learner's developing capacity to reflect on what is known and on one's own learning process. This dimension is possibly the most difficult dimension to collect information about when working with children who are aged under 5. Different theories can be used when looking at this dimension, such as *personal construct* theory, *attribution* theory and *metacognition*. During an assessment we would be gathering information in a variety of ways to answer the following questions: 'What are the child's feelings, attitudes and views of him/herself as a learner and as a person?' and 'Can the child identify likes and dislikes, strengths and weaknesses? If so what does the child do with this information?' Once information has been collected, how can we help young children become more reflective about their experiences? The 'High Scope' approach, to early years education (Brickman and Taylor, 1991) has as part of its daily routine an opportunity for children to talk about what they have done during the session. In a 'High Scope' nursery the 'Plan, Do, Review' cycle is an integral part of each session. A fundamental part of this philosophy is that when children recall their experiences as a regular part of their daily routine the process of looking back becomes more natural to them. 'High Scope' practitioners believe that the first steps for helping children to recall more readily are to encourage children to take the lead in their own activities and then to provide regular times to review their experiences. This process is based on the ideas that young children are capable thinkers and doers, especially when they carry out activities of their own choosing. Review experiences are part of a larger process of planning and by doing this children are offered opportunities to initiate and reflect upon their actions. The process of talking about and representing their actions helps children evaluate and learn from their experiences; it also makes them more capable of drawing upon these experiences in future. The capacity of reflection, fostered in review experiences, is an important foundation for later learning.

Children with a range of special educational needs are able to take an active part in the 'Plan, Do, Review' process, because it does not depend on verbal skills. Children can show models, drawings, paintings or the toys that they have played with and may rely on another child or adult for the language to describe what they have done. This process also gives the children opportunities to hear models of 'good' language.

The use of personal construct theory allows the educational psychologist a way of understanding how a child makes sense of the world and its experiences. With young children the use of drawings and descriptions of a 'happy', 'sad', 'angry' child etc. can give the educational psychologist some insight into a child's understanding of the world and their place in it. It is often thought that young children with communication difficulties have problems reflecting on their environment or their learning; however, detailed observations over time often give an insight into how a child views their experiences. For example, Rumel, a young child at the one-word level of understanding, when about to go from his special nursery class to a mainstream class for integration, jumped up and down, smiling, said 'go to Peterborough' (the name of the nursery). This child was giving staff positive feedback about his experience of integration.

Conclusion

The educational psychologists of Hammersmith and Fulham believe there are many advantages of using the five dimension assessment framework when assessing children who are under 5 with special educational needs. However, assessments using this approach require time, so educational psychologists need to be involved at an early stage with young children and not just at the statutory assessment stage. Often a lot of information is gathered and this can lead to difficulties in summarising the most salient information. Once these issues have been addressed the following advantages outweigh the disadvantages:

- There is an easy structure once it has been internalised.
- It is 'user friendly' with parents, many parents often spontaneously using the same language. One parent said the assessment had 'picked up on Ayesha's little traits' and that the assessment had been fed-back in 'the clearest report'.
- It can be used by educational psychologists irrespective of their theoretical background.
- Nurseries and staff like it as it gives a broad, psychological perspective which fits into the early years curriculum.
- It encourages a systematic look at context-related assessment over time.
- There is a focus on interactional features and not just on 'within' child factors.

The framework matches well with the principles of good practice summarised by Ball (1994) for effective early years education. Thus psychological assessment and intervention are seen to promote a coherent view of the child as a learner within a robust theoretical and practical framework.

References

Ball, C. (1994) *Startright: The Importance of Early Learning*. London: RSA.

Barrs, M., Ellis, S., Hester, H. and Thomas, A. (1990) *Patterns of Learning*. London: Centre of Language in Primary Education.

Boxer, R., Challen, M. and McCarthy, M. (1991) 'Developing an assessment framework: the distinctive contribution of the educational psychologist', *Educational Psychology in Practice*, 7(1), 30–34.

Brickman, N.A. and Taylor, L.S. (eds) (1991) *Supporting Young Learners*. Ypsilanti, Michigan: High/Scope Press.

Bruner, J.S. (1983) *Child's Talk: Learning to Use Language*. Oxford: Oxford University Press.

Donaldson, M. (1978) *Children's Minds*. London: Fontana.

Glachan, M. and Light, P. (1982) 'Peer interaction and learning: can two wrongs make a right?' In Butterworth, G. and Light, P. (eds) *Social Cognition: Studies of Development and Understanding*. Brighton: Harvester.

Haring, N., Lovitt, T.C., Eaton, M.D. and Hansen C.L. (1978) *The 4th R – Research in the Classroom*. Columbus, Ohio: Merrill.

Sylva, K., Roy, C. and Painter, M. (1980) *Childwatching at Playgroup and Nursery School*. London: Grant McIntyre.

Tizard, B. and Hughes, M. (1984) *Young Children Learning: Talking and Thinking at Home and at School*. London: Fontana.

Wood, D. (1991) 'Aspects of teaching and Learning'. In Light, P., Sheldon, S. and Woodhead, M. (eds) *Learning to Think*. London: Routledge/Open University.

Wood, H. and Wood, D. (1983) 'Questioning the Pre-school Child' *Education Review*, **35**, Special Issue (15), 149–62.

Vygotsky, L.S. (1962) *Thought and Language*. Cambridge, Ma.: M.I.T. Press.

Vygotsky, L.S. (1978) In Cole, M., John-Steiner, V., Scribner, S. and Souberman, E. (eds) *Mind in Society: The Development of Higher Psychological Processes*. Cambridge, Ma.: Harvard University Press.

Chapter 12

Surveying Professional Practice in Early Years: Multi-disciplinary Assessment Teams

Hannah Mortimer

Setting the scene

Any family referred for the first time to their local Child Development Centre is likely to meet a confusing variety of professionals. Each will have their own questions, their own models of working, their own theoretical frameworks and their own assessment tools. Even with the very best of intentions and the highest quality of professional training and expertise, there is bound to be confusion and overlap in the eyes of the parents, at least in those first days of hypotheses and planning. Even with the most informative preparatory leaflets, and the clearest of introductions, this is going to be a difficult and potentially threatening time for the parents, and our best endeavours to achieve 'partnership' are at risk.

If professionals are to develop more effective ways of 'dovetailing' their skills within the multi-disciplinary assessment team, then they need to develop a clear understanding of their own unique contribution to the assessment process, and how their skills and roles might overlap with each other. In this chapter, I look at the results of a survey into just these views, and ask the question whether the sum of the whole is more than the sum of the individual parts when considering multidisciplinary assessment.

Before I do so, let us look at the rationale for inter-disciplinary collaboration and the historical backdrop to team work with young children in assessment and intervention. What different models for professional practice have developed in Child Development Centres, what messages of 'power' and 'expertise' do these convey to visiting families, and how do professionals within teams view and support one another?

The historical backdrop

Early years professionals have been exhorted to work more closely together for many years now, and Davie (1993) laments the continuing gap between rhetoric and practice. The National Children's Bureau was first established to promote co-operation in child care, and, through working parties and publications, came to foreshadow the influential Court Report (Court, 1976) and Warnock Report (Warnock, 1978). The Court Report recommended the setting up of multi-disciplinary teams to provide diagnosis, assessment, treatment and education for children with handicaps. The teams suggested consisted of paediatricians, nursing officers, social workers, psychologists and teachers and the service would be provided in locally based Child Development Centres or District Handicap Teams. The Warnock Committee investigated the main requirements for effective assessment, proposing a continuous and staged model involving close collaboration between the professionals concerned. This staged model, with close multi-agency liaison and joint working, has been further developed in the Children Act (Department of Health, 1991) and the Code of Practice (Department for Education, 1994).

The 1980s saw a rapid development of Child Development Centres and District Handicap Teams with a range of clinical functions (Gaussen and Cundall, 1990). Children and families were offered diagnosis and multi-disciplinary assessment of congenital and acquired handicapping conditions, with treatment and intervention. Medical treatment was available, and advice and provision on aids, adaptations and resources. Advice, counselling and support was generally available to parents and families, and information was available on statutory and voluntary services. The Centres were also able to contribute towards advice on the children's special educational needs.

In 1990, I worked with one of the Child Development Services visited by Her Majesty's Inspectorate (HMI) (DES, 1991), and their report makes several references to good practice in interdisciplinary working. In particular, it found that, where provision was less than satisfactory, it was associated with poor co-ordination of the various services available for under-fives, a lack of clear definition in the roles of the workers and an absence of recognised leadership and structures. Joint training opportunities for members of multi-disciplinary teams were encouraged. There were problems of sharing information and maintaining confidentiality when children were seen by a wide range of professionals.

Where the best practice was observed in the organisation and management of services for young children with special needs, several common factors emerged. There was a good balance between individual programming and integration into a peer group, with individual programmes well planned to meet special needs. The multi-disciplinary groups had agreed aims and objectives, with recognition of the importance of individual members' contributions to the team, bearing in mind their expertise. Parents were offered a range of provision with opportunities for choice, including, for example, home visiting, group facilities, nursery provision or playgroups. Professionals involved had the opportunity to provide a continuity of help into school, making the transfer as smooth as possible.

Models for team assessments

We have seen how teams have a wide range of different functions and membership. Another way of classifying team structures is into the manner in which the team members work. Cunningham and Davis (1985) write of 'multi-disciplinary' teams and 'interdisciplinary' teams. The first implies that the child and family might be seen by several specialists, each from different backgrounds and theoretical standpoints. Each might be working in a relatively isolated way from colleagues of other specialisms. However, in an 'interdisciplinary' service, specialists work more closely together, exchanging knowledge with each other, co-ordinating their assessment and interventions, and sharing certain core skills such as counselling, family support and good communication across disciplines, with equal status. Interdisciplinary co-operation depends on team members respecting one another and establishing good working relationships in order to negotiate mutually acceptable goals and actions (Cunningham and Davis, 1985).

A further model of working is the 'transdisciplinary' team. Here, boundaries between disciplines are minimised and the emphasis is upon arena-style assessments and consultation between members to plan approaches which integrate goals from all disciplines (e.g. Bagnato and Neisworth, 1991). This most closely reflects the model which I co-developed during the early 1980s in the Cleveland Preschool Developmental Assessment Clinics (Ross, 1983). Having looked at various models of team assessment, we were particularly keen to share a joint discovery of a child's needs, with parent and professionals equal members of the assessment team. This raised the question of whether our joint observations and discoveries added up to a picture of the whole child which went beyond the sum of the individual assessments.

How members of the assessment team view each other

The *professional* holds a specialised body of knowledge and skills and has undertaken a period of training to acquire them (Dale, 1996). This expertise not only distinguishes and distances the professional from the lay person, but also from members of other professions. The very difference of professional perspective and differing interests can conspire against attempts at a truly transdisciplinary or negotiated approach. The very specialisation of their training can conspire against partnership and a sharing of perceived power with the families. Cunningham and Davis (1985) emphasise the importance of asking how parents themselves construe professionals. This is bound to affect the kind of help they anticipate and, therefore, its perceived usefulness.

Another issue is the level of professionalism and accountability expected of individual team members, perhaps each under separate strands of line management. In any partnership model and team approach, there are opportunities for regular meetings and support with a sharing of those very listening and support skills developed as core roles. Where working relationships are close and run smoothly, there will be continuous opportunity for mutual support and professional peer development.

With so many good reasons for working collaboratively, but so many challenges as well, how do individual team members see each other's roles, and how well do they feel professionally supported by their colleagues?

The survey

I was interested to look at how the various professional roles dovetail together in multi-disciplinary teams which help early years children and their families. In 1995 a questionnaire was devised and sent to 45 child development centres and educational or child development services throughout England and Wales, with a request that copies be passed to each member of their pre-school development team or service. Sixty-six questionnaires were returned in confidence, representing a variety of pre-school services and settings. The majority were returned by child development centres (30%), with educational psychology services (24%), community preschool services (15%) and nursery assessment bases (15%) also well represented. The remainder were from Portage and home visiting services (8%), Social Services departments (3%), and other health service clinics or teams (5%).

The questionnaires represented a cross-section of professionals working with children under 5: educational psychologists ($n=19$), paediatricians (9), physiotherapists (9), pre-school teachers (6), speech and language therapists (6), social workers (4), Portage workers (4), occupational therapists (3), clinical psychologists (2), play therapists (2), a nursery officer and a health visitor attached to a child development service.

Skills and specialities which are unique to each profession

What did respondents feel, in their professional role, were the unique skills and specialities which they brought to the pre-school team that were not offered by other professions? In other words, what are the distinct ingredients of 'educational psychology', or 'occupational therapy', or 'paediatrics' that make each profession distinct and specific in the roles it plays out in the discovery and helping of a young child's special needs? If we can start from a clear description of what each of us provides, then this has to help our accountability to the clients we serve, and provide a clearer idea of how we dovetail and support each other within a multi-disciplinary team. Let us look at each professional group separately.

The role of the pre-school teacher

Teachers saw their role as central at the time of transfer into school, nursery or preschool. They had particular knowledge of the statutory assessment procedures, and were therefore ideally placed to talk families through the process, liaise with schools and education authorities, and set up any introductory visits. Because of their wealth of experience and knowledge of how children learn in a range of settings, they were well placed to complete the educational advice towards statementing of a young child's special educational needs. Once a child was placed in a pre-school setting, their parent liaison role continued, particularly if problems arose, or where nurseries needed advice in setting individual teaching programmes. It was helpful to follow children through at 6-monthly reviews, so that other professionals had the benefit of teaching advice from someone who had known the family and child over the pre-school years. Teachers spoke of their central commitment to integration and inclusion within the team. Quite often, they also had specialist qualifications in teaching children with very particular needs, and this was also especially useful in their role within the team. Some teachers were involved in directly teaching children individually or in small groups, and here they felt their detailed knowledge of both early years approaches and special educational experience to be essential.

The role of the paediatrician

As a doctor, the paediatrician 'offers the unique skill of paediatric and neurological examination, coupled with investigations, and works with parents to identify cause and diagnosis' (verbatim quote). Early diagnosis, counselling and support, perhaps even before referral to the multi-disciplinary team, were felt to be crucial roles. Paediatricians also mentioned their particular role in providing or arranging genetic counselling when necessary, and in tapping into in-patient facilities.

Occasionally, the paediatrician also plays a central assessment and co-ordination role, perhaps providing the definitive *full* developmental assessment, chairing and co-ordinating reviews, and carrying the responsibility for notifying the local education authority that a pre-school child might experience special educational needs in the future. In other teams, these roles were shared or rotated.

Paediatricians also provided the service of monitoring medical condition and needs as the child grew older, and monitoring hearing and vision was an important part of this. Some respondents wore the mantle of a 'voice of experience', 'common sense', 'particular empathy' or 'clout to get things done', though these attributes were also mentioned by other disciplines as very particular to their own professions!

The role of the speech and language therapist

The College of Speech and Language Therapists describes their role as one of offering 'assessment, treatment, advice and counselling to people of all ages with a communication disorder and related eating and swallowing problems. They also offer support and advice to carers such as parents, partners and nursing staff to help them understand the nature of the problem and how they can help' (College of Speech and Language Therapists pamphlet: *Do you need speech and language therapy?*). Our respondents echoed these skills. Most were involved in the assessment and treatment of speech, language and communication disorders, including preverbal skills. Advice was given on feeding, sucking, mouth and tongue movements, and textures of foods. Sometimes, advice on alternative and augmentative communication was necessary, and training was given to other professionals, parents and carers on the use of communication aids and signing systems. Specialist advice was also available on articulatory, phonological and fluency problems in young children.

The role of the physiotherapist

Most of the physiotherapists who replied were specialists in children's work. One service described their role as follows:

> We look at the child as a whole. Our main aim is to work towards helping the child reach his or her maximum potential. Following a thorough assessment and therapeutic diagnosis, the physiotherapist will work closely with parents or carers to establish appropriate goals for the child. This individually planned programme of physiotherapy might cover careful positioning and movement, advice and support, special handling skills, exercise regimes, walking practice, balance and co-ordination exercises, stretches of muscles, chest physiotherapy and equipment needs.

This viewing of the child as a 'whole' was mentioned as particular to various different professions throughout the questionnaires.

The physiotherapists who replied were all involved in the assessment of gross motor skills, and treatment of motor delay. They worked particularly with children with physical disabilities and delay, providing advice on handling and care, lifting, positioning, nasal suctioning, inhibiting abnormal reflexes and advising on splints, boots, braces, wheelchairs and buggies, sometimes with overlap with the occupational therapist. They contributed to team assessments by advising on goals and interventions for motor skills, and were often particularly valuable for the liaison they held with the Special Care Baby Unit. Sometimes, advice was given on the use of therapeutic electrical equipment. Physiotherapists provide stretching and direct physiotherapy, and also give time to passing these ideas to the parents and carers for following through at home. Some physiotherapists also work to help parents relax and avoid the physiological effects of stress.

The role of the occupational therapist

Occupational Therapists work with children of varying ages whose development is interrupted due to physical, psychological or social impairment or disability. They aim to develop the child's maximum level of independence thereby improving practical life skills which hopefully promotes a better quality of life. Work is carried out in conjunction with the child's family or carer in a variety of settings. We assess gross and fine motor skills, writing, independence skills, visual perception and body awareness, and the need for specialised equipment for home and pre-school including seating, wheelchairs, toilet and bathing aids, adaptive equipment to improve everyday skills.

(verbatim quote)

The respondents also mentioned their specialist assessment of switches and information technology. They were also called upon to advise on handedness for a child beginning to write where this was still undetermined.

The role of the clinical psychologist

Some teams had considerable overlap between educational and clinical psychologist with caseload determined by age and stage, or even geographically. In other teams, these respective roles were determined by the availability of the particular psychologist. Clinical psychologists felt that they offered, in particular, family support and counselling, family therapy, cognitive and developmental assessment, advice on behaviour management, and specialist knowledge of certain conditions, such as autism. Occasionally, the clinical psychologist doubled as team manager and facilitator, or even as clinical manager.

The role of the educational psychologist

I asked for more detailed information on the roles and overlaps of educational psychologists, and so relationships with this profession will be described more fully. What, I wondered, was the property which made educational psychology unique to her own profession? Already we have seen, in the way different professionals describe their own 'unique' roles within the multi-disciplinary team, considerable overlap and sharing of skills, roles and attributes.

In its guidance for educational psychologists on the giving of statutory advice to the local education authority, two professional associations ask the question, 'What makes advice psychological?' (AEP/BPS, 1996). Educational psychology advice needs to be based on *scientific methodology*. Psychologists attempt to assist others to find solutions to *difficulties* or *problems* or *needs*. They help by clarifying and defining the problem, generating teaching and management approaches and evaluating the success of these. They have to express this help in the contexts of the relationships and environments which the child experiences, and to draw up advice from an *interactional* and *holistic* viewpoint (their italics).

This specialist approach was mentioned by some respondents, but the majority listed a more general role, with more areas of potential overlap with other professionals. Some felt that their very usefulness arose from their flexible and wide range of knowledge and experience, both in education and in psychology, and the way this was applied. They spoke of providing specialist assessment of cognitive or learning difficulties, providing assessment and advice based on the paradigms of child development and learning theory, and the use and interpretation of normative psychometric assessment. They felt they were particularly well placed to advise on the education system, the resources and provision available and the statutory assessment procedures. Educational psychologists spoke of being able to provide an objective, independent, or non-medical view and to see the child's needs in a wider context than the assessment clinic. They brought particular skills in working with families and in a range of pre-school settings, and they usually had experience of a wide range of special needs and interventions. Advice on behaviour management was often given, and they could help colleagues and parents to focus their observations, and also to make useful interpretations of how the child was playing. Sometimes, specialist skills in bereavement counselling or conflict resolution were called upon.

The role of the social worker

Counselling and family support figured large in these replies, with particular reference to their ability to visit the home, and assess or support the family situation and dynamics. They had access to Social Services provision, including day nurseries, respite care, shared caring, and pre-school support schemes. Again, social workers felt they had a view of the *whole* situation, with an opportunity for managing the 'case' and providing advocacy for the family. Child protection procedures were also mentioned as a crucial and specific role, with the conflict that this can cause with some families.

The role of the Portage worker

Portage is a home-teaching scheme for pre-school children with special needs and their families. Home visitors call regularly to assess where a child has reached in each area of development, to negotiate what to teach next, and to model how to teach it.

Portage workers spoke of the particular benefit of their being able to work on a regular weekly basis with the family in a home setting. This provided them with particular knowledge of the family's needs, and a chance to acknowledge the parents' expertise and value their contribution. They were able to negotiate skills to be taught with the family, break these down into manageable next steps, and thereby encourage the child's motivation and confidence. Moreover, they could highlight learning opportunities in the home, acknowledge the child's need for fun and relaxation, and allow family and child personal choices. Their ongoing and regular contact with the family placed them in a good position to liaise with other members on the team, and provide regular reports on progress.

Is the whole team assessment worth more than the sum of the parts?

The suggestion of the survey is that each professional has certain core skills relating to their specialism and training. However, beyond this, where certain roles are 'dovetailed' within a multi-disciplinary assessment team, the trend is for these roles to be developed by differing professionals depending on each one's particular slant, talent and experience, and on the particular structure in which they work. This makes it as interesting for us to look at the key roles and beliefs which make for 'good practice' and 'ethos' in a whole Child Development Team (e.g. Dale, 1996), as to draw apart the individual professionalisms. In practice, we appear to be encouraging multi-role professionals who have developed a special interest and skill in the assessment and supporting of early years children with special needs and their families. As such, there remains a great deal of cross-boundary thinking and planning still to be done to dovetail the seams. In doing so, we may need to share skills and roles which we had previously felt to be central to ourselves, not least to those families who come to us for help.

Nevertheless, the climate is increasingly one of working together. Children's Services Plans became mandatory for social services departments from April, 1996 in an Order under section 17(4) of the Children Act 1989. Local education authorities, health commissions and trusts, and others all have to be consulted. This provides a real opportunity for agencies and disciplines to plan services for children together, and to have a real voice in designing policy and practice for the future.

References

AEB/BPS (Association for Educational Psychologists and The British Psychological Society Division of Educational and Child Psychology) (1996) *Statutory Advice to the LEA: Guidance for Educational Psychologists.* London: AEB and BPS.

Bagnato, S.J. and Neisworth, J.T. (1991) *Assessment for Early Intervention: Best Practices for Professionals.* London: The Guilford Press.

Court, S.D.M. (Chair) (1976) *Fit for the Future: The Report of the Committee on Child Health Services,* Vol. 1. London: HMSO.

Cunningham, C.C. and Davis, H. (1985) *Working with Parents: Frameworks for Collaboration.* Milton Keynes: Open University Press

Dale, N. (1996) *Working with Families of Children with Special Needs.* London: Routledge.

Davie, R. (1993) 'Interdisciplinary perspectives on assessment'. In Wolfendale, S. (ed.) *Assessing Special Educational Needs.* London: Cassell.

Department of Education and Science (1991) *Interdisciplinary Support for Young Children with Special Educational Needs: A Report by HMI.* Middlesex: DES.

Department for Education (1994) *Education Act 1993: Code of Practice on the Identification and Assessment of Special Educational Needs.* London: HMSO.

Department of Health (1991) *The Children Act 1989: Guidance and Regulations.* London: HMSO.

Gaussen, T. and Cundall, D. (1990) 'Child development centres and district handicap teams – an overview', *Association for Child Psychology and Psychiatry Newsletter,* **12**(3), 3–7.

Ross, H. (1983) 'Parents as partners; preschool assessment in Cleveland', *Parents Voice: Journal of the Royal Society for Mentally Handicapped Children and Adults,* **33**(2),10–11.

Warnock, M. (Chair) (1978) *Special Educational Needs: The Report of the Committee of Enquiry into the Education of Handicapped Children and Young People.* London: HMSO.

Chapter 13

Educational Psychologists and Inter-agency Collaboration for Pre-school Children

Karen Hobson

This chapter considers the changing face of assessment and intervention for pre-school children and the possible role or roles of the educational psychologist (EP) working within a multi-agency framework. It will describe one local education authority's (LEA's) attempts to examine its procedures for assessment and intervention of the under-fives, describe current changes to date, highlight areas for change and implications for further work.

Setting the context for the work of the educational psychologist

EPs hold a psychology degree approved by the British Psychological Society and professional training at Masters degree level. They also have a recognised teaching qualification and a minimum of 2 years teaching experience. Most EPs are employed by LEAs and provide a range of psychological services to children, parents, and teachers, along with other educational, social and health professionals.

There have been a number of legislative changes that have resulted in local authorities needing to examine their current procedures in the area of special educational needs, the most recent being The Education Act 1993 (Section 3) and the corresponding guidelines for its implementation, *The 1994 Code of Practice*. Perhaps for the first time local authorities have not only been told *what* to do, but also given suggestions on *how* to do it, although it can be argued that *The Code* is still open to interpretation by individual authorities and the professionals they employ.

Under Section 176 of the Education Act 1993, health personnel must inform LEA personnel when they have formed an opinion that a child, under the age of 5 years, may have special educational needs. *The Code of Practice* highlights the need for agreed procedures on how this information from health services will be handled to facilitate a speedy response in investigating whether further action needs to be taken by the LEA.

The introduction of a nursery voucher scheme, beginning nationally in April 1997 (see Chapters 1 and 14) will also have an impact on local authority procedures in the assessment and intervention of pre-school children for whom there are concerns about their learning. All voucher-redeeming establishments must have regard to *The Code of Practice*. Therefore establishments which have not previously been required to follow tenets under education law will now be required to do so. Not only does this have massive implications for training but also in setting up monitoring systems in order that procedures, along with record-keeping systems, similar to those required of establishments within the maintained sector of education, are in place.

Principles of good practice

The professional activities of educational psychologists are guided by principles of good practice which have evolved in the light of ongoing research and evaluation. These include:

- assessment in and across contexts
- assessment over time
- working within a preventative framework
- collaborative work with parents and other professionals within a problem-solving framework

(see Sigston et al., 1996; Wolfendale et al., 1992)

Such principles, along with a move from within-child models of assessment to a more holistic view which takes account of a child's range of contexts and experiences, have highlighted the need for EPs to work within a model of joint assessment and active collaboration with both parents and other professionals.

The broadening role of the EP

Whilst the EP's fundamental professional role within local authorities has been, and continues to be, assessment and support of children and young people with long-term and complex special educational needs, there has been, over recent years, an acknowledgement that the EP possesses a range of knowledge, skills and expertise that can take them beyond the role of assessor of individual children. Fox and Sigston (in Wolfendale *et al.*, 1992) detail the EP's role in supporting organisational change, namely within schools, at a systems level, through such interventions as action research e.g. preparing and delivering INSET packages and acting as a facilitator for change through a process consultancy model.

The EP working as consultant at an individual child level can, and does, support schools in advising on particular strategies at stages one and two of the staged assessment procedure. Recently, when schools have had to adopt or modify processes and recording systems for the assessment and observation of children with special educational needs following the guidelines outlined in the *Code of Practice*, they have sought the advice from their visiting EP.

The why, how and when of collaboration

Concepts of 'corporate and collective responsibility' underpin current service provision philosophies (Wolfendale and Wooster; in Pugh. 1996). Phillippa Russell (in Wolfendale *et al.*, 1992) remarks that the concept of joint working with children with special educational needs has been an important principle of any service for some time, not only within education, but across health and social services. She comments that legislation, particularly The Children Act 1989, has led to a growing awareness of interdependence of all services working for children, which has resulted in major challenges for these services in attempting to promote and achieve collaboration and co-ordination. The Education Act 1993 is also underpinned by principles of collaboration between both parents and professionals. Services within local authorities are obliged to work together to provide an integrated service for children and their families, not only as a response to legislation, but also to the increasing climate of public accountability. Collaboration between professionals can take many forms from the individual casework level to senior management policy planning. The EP may collaborate with other professionals in the following ways.

Individual casework

EPs have increasingly worked alongside parents, teachers and other professionals as part of their work with individual children and their families. A crucial component of their assessment is in incorporating the views of others who have direct knowledge of the child.

Working within a multi-disciplinary assessment team

EPs may work as part of a multi-disciplinary assessment team, most commonly within a health setting where the emphasis is on assessment of children under the age of 5 who may have special educational needs. EPs may become involved both prior to, and following formal referral to their service. The EP can bring skills and experience which can complement any team whose work involves the assessment of individual children with special needs by:

- Ongoing joint assessment and planning with parents.
- Providing psychological assessment within an educational context.
- Translating other professionals' assessment into an educational context.
- Assimilating others' views towards providing an holistic picture of an individual child's strengths and difficulties.
- Experience of designing, implementing and monitoring strategies to assist children's learning.
- Knowledge and experience of specific strategies such as Portage.
- A recognition of the importance of setting high, but realistic expectations for children's development in order to promote optimum learning.

Working as part of a co-ordination team responsible for the planning and delivery of under-fives services

Educational psychology services often have natural links with those responsible for policy development within the LEA at a senior management level. Services are often an integral part of the coordination of LEA assessment and planning. They may have established links with other services at a senior management level and are therefore placed in a good position to support co-ordination and collaboration both within education and across other services. EPs' training and experience have enabled them to develop skills in consultation and negotiation, group dynamics, setting agreed aims and objectives, setting and reviewing action plans, drawing on individual's strengths, knowledge of systems work, including action research, and strategies to promote organisational change.

The EP, then, can be seen as an important member of a multi-agency team both at the individual child level and in planning and co-ordinating services at a local authority management level.

The difficulties with collaboration

Despite the rhetoric and professional commitment to collaboration, translating these principles into practice has not proved easy. Maychell and Bradley (1991) comment that whilst finding time for collaboration between professionals is a genuine problem, services need to demonstrate a commitment to inter-agency working through securing time and being flexible. They report that evidence suggests that there has been slow progress in implementing the legislative requirements of inter-agency collaboration. They point to a lack of joint policy development across agencies as one of the main sources of obstruction, making an individual's attempts at collaboration limited despite good intentions. They argue that joint policies would provide a coherent framework which would highlight the importance of collaboration and give support to individual efforts. Development of joint policies would seek to clarify joint aims between agencies and rationalise provision towards providing a more client-centred approach. This can be regarded as particularly important in an increasing climate of public accountability services and budget-led planning.

Maychell and Bradley point out that, in the absence of formal policies, any informal networks that are established are often difficult to maintain once the people who have forged those links move on. They warn that if links are not formalised it is often difficult for new people to tap into existing networks and that leaving the responsibility of collaboration up to individuals is leaving 'too much to chance'.

The context for one local authority

Within the health service a well-established Children's Centre plays a crucial role in highlighting children with probable special educational needs. Following a series of multi-disciplinary play assessment sessions, professionals – including paediatricians, a clinic nurse, health visitor, occupational therapists, speech and language therapists, clinical psychologist and play assistants – will join with parents in a care plan to agree actions that need to be taken, which may, and often does, include a referral to the educational psychology service. Referrals to other education services may also be made, such as the pre-school home visiting service, and/or the service for children with hearing impairment. Prior to an education pre-school project there was no educational input into these sessions although relevant professionals, including those from education, were invited to children's care plans. Often then, decisions about referrals to education services were made in the absence of those working within an educational framework.

The Children's Centre has sought to work collaboratively with other agencies. The EP service has had liaison with the centre over a number of years through regular meetings between a team member and the clinic nurse who acts as co-ordinator for the centre. Within the Children's Centre there is also regular input to the centre from a social worker from the Social Services children and families division.

Referral of children for assessment at the centre is made by parents or any professional when there are concerns about a child's development in two or more areas. Children, for whom there are concerns about only one aspect of their development, are referred directly to the appropriate service.

Referrals to the educational psychology service can be made at any time and by any professional as well as by parents. These can include education support services to whom the centre has initially referred, although the majority of referrals to the service are made directly by the Children's Centre. Referrals for children under the age of 5 may also come to the service through school referrals. There are currently no specific criteria for referral to the service. The section of the education department responsible for special needs (special services) will become involved if a statutory assessment of a child's educational needs is requested.

The local authority Social Services department runs three family centres. Referrals to these can be made by any professional and following the referral an assessment is made to ascertain the appropriateness of a family centre place for that child. Educational professionals visit the family centres if the child has been referred to their service as part of their assessment and intervention.

As with most LEAs there was a need to examine current assessment procedures for all children following the implementation of the Education Act 1993 and the 1994 Code of Practice. Also there had been requests from health and social services personnel for formal links to be made with the educational psychology service towards meeting the needs of pre-school children These requests had come from informal discussions and through more formalised links across the two services. In response to these requests, and the impetus of recent legislation, a pre-school project was started, the aims of which were two-fold:

1. To examine the current interface of liaison and collaboration between and within agencies.
2. To offer a service within a health assessment setting and to social service family centres.

The project had a 'life' of 6 months initially and the co-ordinator was a member of the educational psychology service with an allocation of 1.5 days per week. The key tasks of the specialist pre-school educational psychologist were:

- to manage the LEA's pre-school home visiting team
- to attend assessment sessions at the Children's Centre
- to provide regular consultation sessions at the three family centres run by social services

- to manage the rota and allocation of referrals to the educational psychology service
- to liaise with members of the voluntary sector, the Pre-School Learning Alliance (PLA)
- to provide a training role to the Children's Centre and the family centres
- to feed back to senior management and support the LEA in their response to recent legislation.

Within that time, the specialist EP has attended, and contributed to, assessment sessions at the Children's Centre and has provided training on the requirements within the new Education Act and on the role of an EP. The specialist EP has, by virtue of proximity, been able to liaise with health professionals both on a formal and informal basis. There have been opportunities to discuss the role of the EP and assessment procedures on an informal basis with parents prior to formal referral.

Training has also been given to workers at the family centres and regular consultation sessions have provided the workers with an opportunity to discuss concerns they may have about a particular child and possible actions they may take. Meetings have taken place with the managers of these centres as well as the service manager to elicit their views and to keep them informed of the development of the project.

During the two terms the specialist EP has had regular liaison with other education support services. Discussions have centred on their views on current procedures as well as discussions about individual children. The specialist EP continued membership as an education representative at the education liaison group with voluntary groups, including the co-ordinator of the Equal Chances scheme (PLA) and parents' groups.

The project in terms of commitment of time and proximity to other professionals has facilitated joint working. The use of joint support plans where parents and professionals meet to share their views, offer advice and review short-term targets has been piloted with positive feedback given by all concerned.

The specialist EP has also been involved in ongoing working groups within education to consider changes needed in light of legislation. This has included discussions on introducing phases of assessment for pre-school children, and criteria for statutory assessment for the under-fives, the implementation of both being two of the current key tasks for the specialist EP, along with developing joint support plans and policies for the under-fives. Following the completion of the project it was agreed that the specialist pre-school EP role would continue with an allocation of 2 days per week.

One of the main outcomes of the project has been to initiate discussions about referrals to education support services, particularly in light of Section 176 of the Education Act 1993. The corresponding guidelines in the *Code of Practice* highlight the already existing close co-operation between agencies and the need for the LEA, wherever possible to 'use and build upon this well established network of relationships and services'. The way an LEA responds to 176 notifications (for assessment) from the health authority or health trust sets the tone of collaboration between professionals both prior to and following the notification. Whilst the project identified good practice of collaboration between services and departments, these were, at times, a result of individuals' commitment to collaboration rather than a result of formalised policies and procedures.

Promoting partnership with parents

John Rennie (in Pugh, 1996) remarks on the overwhelming acceptance of the value of parental involvement in work with children, their parents and workers. Within the authority there was a clear commitment to working with parents. All referrals to education support services were made following discussion and agreement by parents. The notification under Section 176 creates a tension between this commitment and health professionals having a duty to inform the LEA when they are of the opinion that a child under the age of 5 may have special educational needs. Any procedures for initiating and responding to 176 notifications will, therefore, need to ensure that parents are given sufficient opportunity to be fully informed of the outcomes of such a notification. Within the authority the specialist EP could play an important role in initial discussions with parents prior to such a notification being made.

Four possible options for an LEA in responding to pre-school referrals

Local authorities vary in terms of how pre-school referrals are made and how the education department responds. For some authorities referrals to the LEA exclusively come through health channels, i.e. through 176 notifications, and may go directly to one particular service for action such as the educational psychology service. The following section describes a number of different local authorities procedures to demonstrate this variance. For the local authority in question, a number of options, including maintaining the status quo, are suggested along with the positive and negative implications each of these may have. Any change to existing procedures will need to be made following close consultation with other services and departments, particularly at a senior management level, and must be considered in the light of existing good practice and established networks. The procedures must also be seen as those that are in the best interests of the child and that optimise partnership with parents.

For each of the four options a SWOT (strengths, weaknesses, opportunities and threats) analysis framework has been used.

Option 1

The present system does not change (Table 13.1)

Strengths	Weaknesses
• Good informal links already established between professionals with a commitment to collaboration • Procedure described as 'parent friendly' • Present referral system is not restricted and bureaucracy is reduced • System reflects currently available time and flexibility of professionals	• Present system can create overlap between services • Little co-ordination and planning between services for the under 5's • No monitoring of LEA provision for the under 5's • Collaboration left up to individuals • Procedures for referral to education not fully in line with *Code of Practice* guidelines • Local procedures can seem complicated for parents and professionals
Opportunities	Threats
• Reaffirms current procedures and networks	• Professionals who have expressed concerns may feel they have not been 'heard'

Table 13.1

Option 2

All pre-school referrals are made directly to the educational psychology service (Table 13.2).

Option 3

All pre-school referrals are made to an education panel led by special services and involving representatives from different education services and other educational professionals with responsibility for under-fives (Table 13.3).

Strengths	Weaknesses
• One service within education responsible for co-ordination and planning and monitoring of educational services at an individual child level • Well-developed links already established with other education services including special services • One service responsible for monitoring of referrals to education • System encourages consistency of referrals	• There may be a delay in children receiving appropriate education services • Department with an overview of special educational provision (special services) has no direct involvement
Opportunities	**Threats**
• EPs become involved at an earlier stage facilitating more proactive work • Encourages earlier links between EP and parents.	• Increased time commitment for the service • Education services may resent EPs 'gate-keeping' their provision • 'Owners' of present system may feel threatened • Informal links may break down, affecting existing good working practices

Table 13.2

Option 4

All pre-school referrals are made to a panel consisting of members from education, health and social services (Table 13.4).

Variations between local authorities

Policies and procedures for supporting children under 5 with special educational needs differ widely from one authority to the next, reflecting the way in which each authority has responded to legislation, which is, in turn, affected by already existing procedures and provision, financial constraints and the priority that under-fives has been given within that authority. Penn and Riley (1992) describe services for young children as 'fragmented', across and within local authorities, differing in both the type and level of service provided. They highlight the vast differences

Strengths	Weaknesses
• Planning and co-ordination of education services at individual child level is facilitated by the LEA • Collaboration between education professionals is encouraged • Procedures fully in line with *Code of Practice* guidelines • System encourages consistency of criteria for referrals to education	• System would create a more bureaucratic process • Parents may be wary of links with a department that deals with special educational provision • Referrers may feel restricted • Referrals may be deferred until referrers feel more certain that a child may have special educational needs to avoid 'special' ball rolling unnecessarily
Opportunities	Threats
• Facilitates the development of a co-ordinated pre-school policy within the LEA with involvement and commitment at a senior management level • Planning and co-ordination of education services for pre school, in general, is encouraged	• 'Owners' of present system may feel threatened • Informal links may break down affecting existing good working practices

Table 13.3

across authorities and call for a need to have more consistent approaches. Pugh (1996) suggests that, while diversity could be a factor of each authority responding differently to differing local needs, it is more likely that it is a result of historical factors along with constraining professional boundaries of providers.

Examples from other authorities

Table 13.5 summarises the key aspect of service delivery for under-fives for four educational psychology services in south east England.

Summary

As policies and procedures for the under-fives differ, so does the role of the EP in terms of the timing and nature of their involvement with under-fives and in their collaboration with other professionals. Despite the differences across LEAs, many members of educational psychology services within specific authorities play an active role in liaising with and

Strengths	Weaknesses
• Collaboration and co-ordination between agencies, promoting joint working at a ground work level • Avoids children 'slipping through the net' • Follows guidelines in *Code of Practice* • System encourages consistency of referrals across agencies and rationalises provision	• System could create delays in children receiving appropriate provision • Parents may be wary of bureaucratic nature of process
Opportunities	Threats
• To develop a local authority under-5's policy • To develop consistent approaches in assessment and intervention of children with special educational needs	• 'Owners' of present system may feel threatened • Increased time commitment • Confidentiality of information

Table 13.4

working alongside other professionals. This encompasses the whole range of involvement from an individual child level to decision making and policy development at a senior management level. Local authorities need to engage in an informed debate on the available options with the aim of developing policies and procedures which encourage a 'collective and corporate responsibility'.

LEA	Focus of Service Delivery
A	• Under-5's team of five psychologists participating in multi-disciplinary assessment and contributing to the planning for children following assessment • Children are notified exclusively through health channels • Head of under-5's team involved in the planning for pre-school children within the education department • Educational psychology services under-5's policy highlights a commitment to liaising closely with other professionals involved
B	• Senior EP with responsibility for under-5's: attending meetings on policy making for the under-5's across departments and attending a day care panel co-ordinated by social services • Referrals to EP service through section 176 notification from health personnel forwarded by LEA special services department and through pre-school assessment referrals which are forwarded directly to the educational psychology services
C	• Senior EP with responsibility for under-5's and has an overview of all pre-school referrals • Referrals to the educational psychology service are forwarded by the special needs section of the local education authority and come via 176 notifications, parents and other professionals • Senior EP is a member of a pre-school panel which decides an appropriate action following referral to education and includes representatives from the special needs section, schools, social services and health. Referrals are made through 176 notifications by parents and by other professionals • No formal under-5's policy within the educational psychology services. Liaison with parents and professional is an expectation. • Senior EP is a member of an education under-5's planning group: future plans include involving health and social services personnel • Educational psychology service is represented on a borough-wide Children's Services planning group
D	• Children notified exclusively through 176 notifications from the health authority • Formalised stages of assessment highlight collaboration with parents and other professionals at each stage • Liaison group for under-5's within the educational psychology service responsible for developing under-5's initiatives and policies.

Table 13.5

References

Department for Education (1994) *Code of Practice on the Identification and Assessment of Special Educational Needs*. London: HMSO.

Maychell, K. and Bradley, J. (1991) *Preparing for Partnership: Multi-agency Support for Special Needs*. Windsor: National Foundation for Educational Research.

Penn, H. and Riley, K.A. (1992) *Managing Services for the Under 5's*. London: Longman.

Pugh, G. (ed.) (1996) *Contemporary Issues in the Early Years: Working Collaboratively for Children* (2nd edn.). London: Paul Chapman.

Sigston, A., Curran, P., Labram, A. and Wolfendale, S. (eds) (1996) *Psychology in Practice with Young People, Families and Schools*. London: David Fulton Publishers.

Wolfendale, S., Bryans, T., Fox, M., Labram, A. and Sigston, A. (eds) (1992) *The Professional and Practice of Educational Psychology: Future Directions*. London: Cassell.

Chapter 14

'All Young Children Have Needs'

Jo Goodall

Introduction

Within the context of good practice for nursery children I shall explore principles underpinning quality nursery education as the basis for helping children with SEN, valuing the potential of nursery education to support all young children's development and especially those with SEN as emphasised in The Warnock Report:

> We recommend that the provision of nursery education for all children should be substantially increased as soon as possible, since this would have the consequence that opportunities for young children with special needs could be correspondingly extended.
>
> (Warnock, 1978:87)

It is salutary to remember that inclusive education for young children is a relatively recent phenomenon, and is still developing. For those practitioners working in nursery education with a specific brief for young children with SEN, the fundamental characteristics of early childhood education are gradually becoming more prominent in practice. The preoccupation with and focus upon a child's SEN has for some providers been a predominant concern, with a skills-based curriculum of paramount importance. Many OFSTED reports (especially those of specialist nursery classes and special school nurseries) have commented on the lack of equal opportunities, rigid curriculum constraints, inappropriate resourcing, inaccessible environments and the absence of play as an integral part of teaching and learning.

Current concerns about the general context of nursery education include major changes such as the implementation of nursery vouchers and statutory duties to 'have regard' to the *Code of Practice* and the *Quality Assurance Framework* (DFEE, 1996a).

Nursery education

Nursery Education is a term beset with difficulties in its interpretation in practice. Confusion occurs in deciding the age range to which it pertains, the content and quality of the education provided, and by whom it is provided. Practitioners have a diverse range of qualifications and experience. Also, misconceptions occur regarding the wide variety of environments providing nursery education. The Rumbold Committee commented: 'Education for the Under-fives can happen in a wide variety of settings and can be supplied by a wider range of people' (DES, 1990; p.11, Note one).

Legislation has not supported a cohesive approach towards implementing nursery education. Provision has evolved on an *ad hoc* basis frequently through local authority initiatives and those developed by voluntary and private sectors. Availability and access to quality nursery education is a 'lottery' for many children and families.

The importance of nursery education has been promoted with an array of arguments in its favour, including supporting a child's development during a period of profound growth (Brierley, 1984); the amelioration of social disadvantage; providing a basis for longitudinal academic achievements; and the advancement of inclusive education (Warnock, 1978).

Principles of nursery education

Nursery education has fundamental principles which must underpin practice, based upon the characteristics of young children, acknowledging differences in life experiences and physical, personality and developmental states. Practitioners should take into account and capitalise upon the Twelve Principles outlined in the *Start Right* report (Ball, 1994).

Other crucial features supporting quality nursery education include:

- A clear management structure which supports and facilitates the work of well-qualified, knowledgeable and sensitive early years staff through:
  - developing policies;
  - monitoring and evaluating practice;
  - promoting opportunities for professional development;
  - ensuring staff have clear knowledge of their roles and responsibilities;
  - regular reviews and opportunities for team building, where each member is valued and included.
- High adult:child ratios which support a child-centred approach to learning and the flexibility to respond to individual children's needs.

This is important when providing a developmentally appropriate curriculum, requiring time to learn about each child, his or her family context and to plan with them meaningful, enjoyable and motivating play opportunities.

- A curriculum framework which develops learning experiences, building upon a child's knowledge and current achievements, fostering positive attitudes to learning and requiring regular skilled observations to facilitate planning, assessment procedures and record keeping.
- Accommodation and resources both inside and outside which are safe and hygienic and promote good health, appropriate to the needs of young children in terms of access, active learning and sensory exploration. Environments and resources should be welcoming, pluralistic, challenging and varied, whilst supporting opportunities for children's social and communication skills to be developed. Additionally, internal and external environments should be identifiable by children for specific activities with plentiful materials, labelled differentially, stored accessibly, with facilities for display and clear pathways for movement.
- A partnership which:
  - acknowledges, celebrates and capitalises on parent or carer involvement, as the child's first educator;
  - is flexible, negotiated and responsive to the needs of individual parents/carers and their families;
  - provides opportunities whereby nursery colleagues offer parents or carers a range of options;
  - is centred upon their own child, themselves, their families and their community;
  - allows them to become active partners in their child's education.
- A strong belief in and commitment to multi-agency working, where:
  - knowledge of other agencies' practice is well known and incorporated into nursery education, including shared training, advice and support for children, families and colleagues;
  - opportunities to liaise with networks and other contacts and procure resources; involvement in assessment procedures;
  - community initiatives;
  - local authority reviews and planning schedules.
- An ethos where all children are valued, involved and sensitively challenged to explore their individual potential.

These features are central to quality nursery education, correlating with statutory duties under legislation (1989 Children Act; 1990 Community Care Act; 1993 Education Act; 1995 Disability Discrimination Act). The responsibilities under these Acts to provide for young children with SEN have in practice been variably interpreted and implemented. Parental perspectives are illuminating:

I was so pleased my health visitor suggested I spoke to an Educational Psychologist about nursery education for my child with cerebral palsy. The nursery's admission policy meant a place was available and at an under-5s planning meeting, there were people from other agencies, and I was able to explain the types of support I felt my child needed.

If only I had known he could have gone to a nursery and had help. I knew his behaviour was different but I thought maybe by the time he goes to school, things will be alright. I am so angry and sad an opportunity has been lost.

(Comments by two parents at a parent/carer workshop on SEN)

Parental awareness of available nursery education can still be dependent upon chance information and locational factors. The widespread provision envisaged for young children with SEN through mandatory, collaborative working practices is slow to emerge. Influences on implementation include the plethora of government agencies involved; the restructuring of departments; reduction in personnel; diversity in discretionary and statutory duties; emergent general agreement and coherent response to legislative terms such as 'Children in Need' and 'Children with SEN'.

Nursery vouchers and their impact

These issues are unlikely to diminish once the new Nursery Education and Grant Maintained Schools Act 1996 comes into effect. For LEAs the impact on strategic planning and financial management was commented upon in the Audit Commission Report on Nursery Education:

The scheme poses for Local Authorities twin challenges of sustaining their funds in a competitive environment and sustaining goodwill among all organisations working with Under Fives.

(1996:42)

Accompanying the new Nursery Education Act, guidance for parents states:

The nursery education scheme is for all 4 year olds, including those with Special Educational Needs.

(DfEE, 1996:10)

Parents will be entitled to exchange a voucher worth (currently) £1,100 for three terms of education from April 1997 through 'flexible options' from a variety of providers.

There are implications for co-ordinating and exchanging vouchers across the range of nursery education a young child with SEN may be involved in. These include home teaching schemes, specialist or other playgroup provision, and/or a nursery placement. For maintained nursery providers much of the information provided by the DfEE regarding the Nursery Voucher Scheme and the *Code of Practice* is not unfamiliar, although there are widespread fundamental concerns about the implementation of the scheme for all young children.

All pre-school provisions within Phase 1 of the Scheme are identified as 'nurseries'. This information is potentially misleading as parents cannot presume that their children with SEN will be supported appropriately and have access to the educational practice described earlier. The emphasis of the scheme is educational, although providers may have focused upon daycare, child and family guidance, counselling and therapeutic support. Their ability to 'diversify' is questionable, not least because the services to be offered and the resources for implementation remain unspecified. One playgroup leader responded:

> At present under the 1989 Children Act we were only given loose guidelines as to our curriculum provision, the Social Services criteria being more for the care rather than education of the child. With the implementation of the voucher system, we will be working to the 'desirable outcomes' detailed in the SCAA Report.

Establishments which apply to redeem vouchers have through validation to provide details regarding their provision for children with SEN (DfEE, 1996c, Annexes B and C). They are also obliged to teach an educational programme focused upon 'Desirable Outcomes', to publish information for parents and to be inspected regularly. The Nursery Voucher Scheme has drawn attention to early years education affecting all children. The messages however are not necessarily those early years educators would wish to have promoted.

Vouchers will not necessarily increase quality nursery provision for all children and rural areas have specific needs not accounted for within the scheme. For all children, parents may be under the misapprehension that the voucher will guarantee their child a nursery place. For children with SEN whose requirements may include extra adult support, adaptations and individual resources, it is unlikely the voucher will be sufficient to cover the actual costs, and this funding shortfall could preclude their admission to a nursery.

Nursery vouchers and special needs

The Special Educational Consortium, under the auspices of the Council for Disabled Children had major reservations about the Nursery Voucher Scheme and the possible problems for young children with SEN. These were considered by the DfEE as part of their proposals. The issues below have been extended from the Consortium's original concerns:

- Lack of time for a proper evaluation of the first phase of the scheme, particularly with regard to nursery provision for children with SEN.
- Local authorities could be pressurised to supplement finance for children with SEN in an array of private and voluntary nurseries. However, local authorities would not necessarily have any involvement in admissions policies or management issues, other than to monitor children who were statutorily assessed. The expectation for financial support could occur at a time when local authorities are more inflexible and in a less secure budget situation (not least because of the revenue retrieved by central government from LEAs to implement vouchers).
- Nursery opportunities for 3-year-old children with SEN might decline in face of the attractions of accepting 4 year olds with vouchers.
- Parents might attempt to secure preferred nursery provision, additional funding or resources by requesting statutory assessment which could ultimately put pressure on 'overstretched' departments. In some nursery settings this could also lead to inappropriate, premature 'labelling', negating young children's different rates of development and stages of maturity, and resulting in underestimation of the children's ability to learn and a narrowing of their educational opportunities.
- New providers face a very steep learning curve regarding young children with SEN and their individual requirements. Inability to shoulder fully their responsibilities to resource support and provision may force them to limit inclusive education opportunities.
- The Code does not solve the problems of 4 year olds with SEN finding themselves in inappropriate provision.
- The Code does not prevent the deregulation of premises from affecting adversely those young children with SEN who require more space for mobility, pathways, storage and privacy.
- The Code of Practice should be applied immediately in all nurseries when the second phase of the voucher scheme is introduced from April 1997.
- Professional development has not been fully addressed in the introduction of the Voucher Nursery Scheme.

There are significant staff training implications for new institutions seeking to redeem vouchers, not least in the numbers of personnel. Appropriate training will be required for all nursery staff, governors, proprietors, and managers. The prior knowledge, expertise and interest in the education of young children with SEN is likely to be extremely variable and training will need to reflect this fact. The urgency for immediate training cannot be overestimated as otherwise children with SEN will attend nurseries where there are few, if any, qualified and experienced staff. Every effort should be made to avoid placing these children in such a vulnerable situation.

The Code of Practice has been an influence upon maintained nursery practice since September 1994, when opportunities were provided for inservice training. This usually occurred through organising supply cover and utilising professional training days. For new nurseries there may be insufficient funds to cover supply costs and the option to close a nursery may not be viable. Releasing staff for training whilst others 'cover' the children, may place the institution in breach of statutory ratios.

Training needs

The DfEE envisages that any nursery wishing to redeem vouchers will use a proportion of that funding to support professional development. To ensure that professional development is incorporated into working practice for all nurseries participating in the scheme, inspectors will consider whether the training that has been organised actually promotes staff knowledge and develops skills in special needs education. Inspectors should also consider nurseries' memberships of organisations and subscriptions to periodicals and magazines which support their professional awareness about SEN education. Concerns about training are not just the province of nurseries themselves. The Special Educational Consortium expressed grave reservations about the knowledge-base and individual qualifications of inspectors were sufficient to assess provision for young children with SEN. The Consortium emphasised their view that current inspector training was insufficient and the inspection schedule too limiting to permit realistic analysis and informed judgements on a nursery's provision for SEN.

Implicit in any quality training initiative must be the finance required. The notion that a voucher realistically covers the diversity of training required to familiarise practitioners with the Code of Practice has been acknowledged by the DfEE, as in this quotation from an interview with a DfEE spokesperson in August, 1996:

> The option the DfEE is currently exploring to fund training for the Code of Practice and its application in nurseries redeeming vouchers is via GEST. However, GEST historically has been co-ordinated by Local Education Authorities and if this was to remain, new conditions would be applied, including 'open enrolment' on courses to include non-maintained nurseries.

Duties remain under The Children Act (1989) and The Education Act (1993) for local authorities to provide information to those involved in caring for, and educating children with SEN. New nurseries, unfamiliar with the Code of Practice, may make increased demands on the statutory authorities for advice and support. They may envisage this in the form of opportunities for staff training.

Training requires a consistent, coherent approach by qualified trainers who have a sound knowledge base of child development, quality nursery education and a professional expertise in supporting young children with SEN.

Possibilities for a future training framework could be the positive development of multi-agency training teams, promoting a shared perspective of assessment, parent/carer partnership; strategies for organising environmental, resource and curriculum provision and child development. Under Fives Fora, and Under Eights Fora could take a lead role in supporting nurseries in their practice and provision for young children with SEN.

Training for all nursery staff in working with parents or carers is crucially important. Particular skills to be learnt include how to broach and explore with parents/carers the nursery's view that their child may have special educational needs. This requires skill and knowledge about strategies to promote parental involvement in assessment procedures and to explain what the nursery's provision for their child will be. Training in equal opportunities for practitioners working with parents or carers and their children is also extremely important. This includes sensitive support and informed consideration, especially for adults who have English as an additional language or experience a disability themselves. Training should also support nursery staff in recognising and maintaining professional and personal boundaries. This could include familiarisation with other agencies which may be more skilled in counselling or have particular expertise in aspects such as finance or advocacy.

It is feasible to develop existing Parent Partnership Schemes within LEAs to participate in training for nursery colleagues.

Successful implementation of the *Code of Practice* will require high-quality training which challenges practitioner's perceptions of parents, promotes interpersonal relationships and develops communication skills.

Practical concerns

For the Code of Practice to be implemented successfully by new nurseries, there must be very thorough support and explanatory advice about administrative procedures and the documentation associated with the assessment process. This may involve some nurseries considering storage, confidentiality and reprographic costs. A playgroup supervisor commented: 'Playgroups run on a very tight budget cannot afford printing costs and rely on parents and friends who may have access to office equipment.'

This raises concerns for the future about access to children's records and details of assessment. Unless training provides clear guidance about administration and examples of proformas for the assessment process, there could be wide variations in the way nurseries devise procedures, leading to an incoherent information exchange between agencies. A local authority nursery headteacher, involved in assessment procedures remarked: 'I have received a booklet from the Local Education Authority on guidance for assessment. There are eleven pages of notes, some of which are helpful, then a further nine pages of proformas. I feel as if implementing the Code of Practice for young children is a paper nightmare.'

Assessment responsibilities

This headteacher had the SENCO responsibility within her nursery. Her comment reflects the complexities in record keeping for the assessment process. (School based Summary Stages One to Three 2:120 *Code of Practice*.) For nurseries redeeming vouchers the responsibility of implementing the *Code of Practice* requires each to have a SENCO (2:14 *The Code of Practice*). This post could be held by a manager, supervisor, proprietor or headteacher or could be delegated to a member of staff. The SENCO role includes:

- assisting in the development and practical application of a nursery policy on SEN
- providing advice and support to colleagues
- record keeping and the placement of children with SEN on a specific nursery register
- liaison with parents/carers and external agencies
- organisation of Stages One to Three procedures of the Code of Practice
- initiating Statutory Assessment.

Without substantial training and support, new nursery SENCOs unfamiliar with the *Code of Practice* (particularly Section 5: Assessment and Statements for Under Fives), its terminology, philosophy and procedures could inadvertently place young children with SEN at risk. The proposed additional guidance by the DfEE to assist new nurseries to interpret the *Code of Practice* pragmatically will promote a better understanding of procedures. However it will not negate the concerns of early years' groups about the use of assessment in a wide range of environments, applied by practitioners whose knowledge-base on the subject of assessment is equally variable.

For some, assessment will be a new concept and their awareness of strategies and the rationale for assessment will be limited. Training which emphasises the need for sensitive collation of information from parents or carers and others involved in a child's life prior to entering a nursery will be crucial. This initial 'assessment data', pertinent to individual children, will be directly relevant to the planning of nursery provision. It needs to be reinforced as a precursor to any more formal assessment procedures. Training has to stress that any assessment involves an overall approach to children's development, their relationships, their knowledge and their abilities: it should also emphasise opportunities to involve the children in the process. SENCOS will also need to develop their practice through training in the use of assessment strategies, their suitability and interpretation, including checklists, developmental tests, observations and medical diagnosis. They need to be alerted to assessment procedures, the timing, the place, the assessment structure and the ultimate use of information obtained. They require knowledge of multi-professional assessment, organisation of Stages Four and Five of the the *Code of Practice* and the necessity to respond to other legislation governing assessment practice. In all their work, 'Account should be taken of the particular needs of the child such as health, disability, religious persuasion, cultural and linguistic background.'(The Children Act, 1989:18)

The underpinning principles for the use of assessment within the context of high quality early years education is described by Mary Jane Drummond and Cathy Nutbrown (1996). They explore 'respect', 'education and care', 'the use of loving power' and the 'interests of the child being paramount'. SENCOs will require this knowledge because of their pivotal role in assessment in nurseries, and the need to advise and to challenge colleagues' assumptions about children with SEN. They need to guard against the dangers of under- or overestimating children's ability to learn and the consequent provision of inappropriate play opportunities.

Children's needs

Training should include the organisation of a system of Individual Education Programme (IEP), a requirement within the the *Code of Practice* (2:93). *In the Nursery Education Scheme: Next Steps* (DfEE, 1996c) the basis of an IEP will incorporate learning outcomes.

The appropriateness of learning outcomes for all 4–5-year-old children has been debated at length. The suggestion that outcomes are within the 'normal range' and appropriate for these children to learn is hotly contested, particularly the methods by which they may be taught and the skills, knowledge and qualification of those who will 'teach'.

The potential for practitioners to design IEPs which are narrowly focused upon the acquisition of skills or the structuring of play so that it reduces a child's involvement and motivation could ironically undermine their very purpose. Unless training is given which facilitates practitioners' awareness that IEPs ought to revolve around a child learning through their senses, with a variety of materials, utilising inside and outside environments and promoting first-hand experience and active involvement, the opportunities for inclusive education will be limited.

Training must explore these aspects with practitioners implementing IEPs, so that they do not supersede spontaneous learning. It must reinforce the essential role of adult practitioners facilitating learning by observing children and following their lead with sensitive and developmental interventions. Training should also support strategies for practitioners to use with young children whose SEN may make it harder for them to initiate and sustain an interest in play, and/or communicate, and/or socialise.

Irrespective of the Nursery Voucher Scheme and its implications, including adherence to the the *Code of Practice*, high-quality play, communication and socialisation remain integral for *all children* in good early years education.

References

Ball, C. (1994) *Start Right: The Importance of Early Learning*. London: Royal Society of Arts.

Breedlove, C. and Schweinhart, J. (1982) *The Cost Effectiveness of High Quality Early Childhood Programs*. Ypsilanti, Michigan: High Scope Educational Research Foundation.

DfEE (1994) Circular 6/94: *The Organisation of Special Educational Provision*. London: HMSO.

DES (1990) *Starting with Quality*. London: HMSO.

DfEE (1996b) *The Implementation of the Code of Practice for Pupils with Special Educational Needs*. London: HMSO.

DfEE (1996a) *Nursery Education: Desirable Outcomes for Children's Learning on Entering Compulsory Education*. London: HMSO.

DfEE (1996c) *Nursery Education Scheme: Next Steps*. London: HMSO.

Drummond, M.J. and Nutbrown, C. (1996). In Pugh, G. (ed.) *Contemporary Issues in the Early Years* (2nd edn). London: Paul Chapman Publishers.

OFSTED (1995a) *The OFSTED Framework for the Inspection of Schools*. London: HMSO.

OFSTED (1995b) *The OFSTED Handbook: Guidance on the Inspection of Nursery and Primary Schools*. London: HMSO.

Pugh, G. (ed.) (1996) *Contemporary Issues in the Early Years Working Collaboratively for Children* (2nd edn). London: Paul Chapman.

Warnock, M. (Chair) (1978) *Special Educational Needs: Report of the Committee of Enquiry into the Education of Handicapped Children and Young People*. London: HMSO.

Wolfendale, S. (ed.) (1997) *Working with Parents of Children with SEN after The Code of Practice*. London: David Fulton Publishers.

Chapter 15

Inclusive Education for Children with Special Educational Needs in the Early Years

Chris Lloyd

Introduction

The purpose of this chapter is to explore two themes relating to early years education and special educational needs (SEN). The first and central theme is:

> that the principles which inform early years education can be seen to provide for the whole of education a model of genuine inclusion, for those children identified as having SEN.

The second theme, closely related and inherently at odds with the first, is:

> that current pressures on and changes in education policy, with regard to the curriculum for the early years, can affect detrimentally those principles, leading to more exclusion for those children identified as having SEN.

Central to the exploration of both themes is the issue of inclusion. It is important to begin by defining what is meant by inclusion, in this context, and by discussing its value and importance to those children identified as having SEN.

Inclusion for children with SEN

The Warnock Report (DES, 1978) clearly stated that children with SEN should be entitled to an equal educational opportunity.

> 'The purpose of education for all children is the same; the goals are the same.'
> (DES, 1978, 1:4)

and

> . . . education as we conceive it is a good and specifically human good, to which all humans are entitled.
>
> (DES, 1978, 1:7)

and

> . . . although the difficulties which some children encounter may dictate what they have to be taught, the disabilities of some how they may be taught, the point of their education is the same.
>
> (DES, 1978, 1:10)

The Report also asserted that integration was the central contemporary issue in special education and should be seen as the major means for ensuring entitlement to an equal educational opportunity for children with SEN.

The Warnock Report, for all its shortcomings, focused a great deal of attention on the educational needs of disabled young people and directed attention to how the mainstream of educational provision might be responsible for addressing those needs. Subsequent education legislation, in the 1981, 1988 and 1993 Education Acts, has reaffirmed that, wherever possible, children with SEN should be educated within the mainstream of educational provision if they are to have access to an equal educational opportunity.

It has become accepted wisdom that integration was 'a good thing' – to be striven towards wherever possible. Indeed the *Code of Practice* (DfEE, 1994) includes as one of its fundamental principles:

> The needs of most pupils will be met in the mainstream . . . . Children with special educational needs, including children with statements of special educational needs, should . . . . be educated alongside their peers in mainstream schools.
>
> (DfEE, 1994, para. 1:2)

Many educationalists, writers and disabled people themselves – working, researching and writing in the area – have, however, become disenchanted with this notion. They have begun to articulate the need for an alternative, or, at the very least, for the discourse which has developed around integration to be deconstructed and reconstructed into a more meaningful concept (Barton, 1989; Lloyd, 1994; Oliver, 1990, 1992; Reiser and Mason, 1990; Tomlinson, 1986).

Oliver (1992) makes a powerful case for the redefinition and reconstruction of what he calls the 'old view' of integration into a 'new view', informed by a notion of full participation in society as a human right, which he sees as being necessary for full inclusion. The concepts of integration and inclusion cannot be seen as interchangeable or synonymous, although they are often used in such a way in practice. They are significantly different in their essential meaning for they are informed and underpinned by very different views, or models, of disability. Inevitably, therefore, they demand very different solutions in terms of educational provision.

It is possible to identify three models of disability informing educational policy, provision and practice (Lloyd, 1994; Oliver, 1992, 1994) the adoption of different models leads to different interpretations of the concept of integration. The first of these models, and the one which has traditionally informed educational thinking with regard to disability, can be described as a medical model. Disability is seen as a problem or personal tragedy (Barton and Oliver, 1992) located within the individual that can be 'cured', at least in part, by some sort of treatment. The disability rather than the person becomes the central focus for concern. In terms of integration the question posed is; 'Is the child good enough for the school/education system?'

Where the answer is 'No', measures must be taken to remediate the deficits of the child in order that she or he can become sufficiently 'normal' to fit into the school or education system. In terms of educational provision this approach finds expression in withdrawal groups or special classes, and where the normalisation process fails the final solution is segregation in special schools.

The second model recognises the handicapping effects of the context in which the child operates. This model can be seen to underpin the recommendations of the Warnock Report and has, since the early 1980s, informed much education policy and provision. In terms of integration the question posed is: 'Is the school or education system good enough for the child?'

Where the answer is 'No', measures must be taken to provide extra resourcing to compensate for the deficiencies of the school or education system. In terms of educational provision this approach finds expression in additional class support and assistance to cope within the mainstream curriculum.

Both models are clearly rooted in notions of disability as deficit, to be normalised; and both rely on compensatory approaches to enable the child to have access to the mainstream of education. In neither case, however, is the mainstream provision itself placed seriously under scrutiny. The assumption is that the mainstream of education and its curriculum offer access to a genuine and equal opportunity for all, with measures taken to remediate or compensate for any deficits which hinder or prevent that access. Where those measures are unsuccessful, the provision of segregated education is considered a legitimate alternative. This view is challenged by many (Barton and Landeman, 1993; Oliver 1992;

Tomlinson, 1986) who regard the current mainstream of education as being exclusive, competitive and indeed irrelevant to all but a small minority of pupils – and for those with SEN – for the most part totally inappropriate. Kelly, looking at the whole issue of entitlement and its implications, especially in relation to the early years, is extremely critical about current attempts to claim that the mainstream curriculum meets the necessary criteria of access to an equal opportunity for all (Kelly, in Blenkin and Kelly, 1994).

Another closely related issue, totally ignored by these remedial or compensatory approaches, is the point made in the Warnock Report itself that the dominant mainstream curriculum has the potential to *create* SEN, and that school-based factors can actually cause or aggravate children's difficulties.

Disenchanted and dissatisfied with the limited access to a genuine educational opportunity for children with SEN, disabled people themselves are currently proposing a third model (Oliver, 1994; Reiser and Mason, 1990). This can be seen as an equal-opportunities, human-rights model. Here the question posed in terms of educational provision is:

> How can integration be achieved in an unequal society? What are the consequences of integrating children into an education system which reflects and reinforces those inequalities?
>
> (Barton and Oliver, 1992:79)

These questions raise highly problematic issues about current education policy, provision and organisation. If a genuinely equal educational opportunity for all children is to be seriously addressed, the whole of education must be planned and conceived from a different perspective, insisting on a 'new view' of integration which

> . . . rejects totally any ideas about normalisation or compensation in provision for disabled people . . . . The demand is for an inclusive approach to all planning and provision. There is a recognition too of the value of celebrating and capitalising on the enrichment of difference and diversity rather than the impoverishment of provision through the process of fitting it to a narrow set of artificially produced concepts of what is normal.
>
> (Lloyd, 1994:187)

The issues raised here require far more attention than the scope of this chapter permits. However, educational provision predicated on notions of inclusion as a human right or entitlement requires that individual difference and diversity are regarded as enrichment rather than as deficit, and that children are sufficiently empowered by their curriculum to participate fully in that education as equal partners.

Early years education as a model of inclusion

Do the principles underpinning early years education provide a model for genuinely inclusive education? Blenkin (1994) identifies four principles on which early years education is founded, which can be summarised as follows:

- Education is defined in terms of processes, planned in relation to individual development.
- Affective, cognitive and psychomotor development are seen as intrinsically linked and interrelated.
- The social context in which early learning takes place is of crucial importance.
- The role of play in learning and development is vitally important.

She goes on to point out that the early years are a period of rapid learning and development, a point also made in the Warnock Report at the beginning of Chapter 5, 'Children Under Five'.

Blenkin also emphasises the importance of the role played by adults in the learning process, again a theme which is stressed in Chapter 5 of the Warnock Report and indeed throughout the entire report. The final critical element in the early learning of children is, for Blenkin, the opportunity to experience a rich variety of practical and play activities which are essential for the encouragement of creativity.

These principles are endorsed by Bruce (1987) who identifies 10 common principles which have traditionally informed the development of early childhood education and which, in her view, continue to be essentially the framework for current practice. Paraphrased, these are:

- Childhood is seen as valid in itself – it is not simply a preparation for adulthood.
- The whole child is centrally important.
- Everything in learning links, interconnects and it cannot be compartmentalised.
- Intrinsic motivation and self-directed activity are highly valued goals of early learning.
- There are specially receptive periods of learning at different stages of development.
- What children *can* do rather than what they *can't* do is the starting point.
- Children have an inner creativity and imagination which emerges given certain favourable conditions.
- Social interaction, especially with adults, is vitally important.
- Education is the interaction between the child and the environment, knowledge and other persons.

These principles are totally compatible with the model of education proposed in the previous section as offering opportunities for genuine inclusion. They begin with the learning processes of the child, recognising different rates of development and making allowance, therefore, for the widest range of abilities. Indeed, as the starting point is what the child *can* do rather than what she or he *cannot* do, there are inevitably more possibilities to include a wider range of difference and diversity from the onset. The view of adults as enablers, responsible for structuring and managing a challenging and stimulating learning environment which emphasises opportunities for creativity and play, as well as a rich variety of personal interactions, is also compatible with an inclusive view of education. There are opportunities within this approach for capitalising on difference and diversity and for laying emphasis on a very wide range of possible abilities and skills.

> If we could imagine an education regime in which development of character, the handling of emotions and personal interactions were genuinely valued as central, in which plenty of time was devoted to them and in which a serious attempt was made to foster and assess them, then what we count as normal . . . would turn out very different from what we do today.
>
> (Wilson and Cowell, 1986:57)

These ideas proposing an alternative to the educational provision found in the majority of mainstream schools and broadening the possibilities for including more children with SEN, are clearly to be found within the principles of early years education.

In emphasising as important goals, self-motivation and self-directed activity, early years education can be seen as working towards the empowerment of its charges, previously mentioned as a prerequisite for genuine participation and inclusion in education. Recognition of the importance of play and practical experience as means for learning, and of the need to emphasise the cognitive, affective, creative and psychomotor, development of the whole child, also offers opportunities for more inclusion. This broad and balanced approach to learning and development offers the possibility for what is counted as success and achievement to be expanded and for the widest range of abilities to be included.

The value of effective, high-quality early years education has long been recognised by educationalists, politicians, parents and all of the concerned agencies:

> By any account, and looking back over a long line of research, early childhood education certainly *pays off* handsomely. It very often provides the meaningful opportunities for play, for social response, for burgeoning confidence to operate. It lays the foundation for the pro-social, and probably for cognitive, behaviour necessary in later schooling.
>
> (Gammage, 1992:10)

For children identified as having SEN it can be seen as doubly crucial. It offers, in addition to the opportunities mentioned above, the possibility for them to develop at their own pace within a carefully managed and structured learning environment which is designed to recognise and support success and achievement in their widest sense. It allows different abilities to be valued and assessed in relation to the child's own growth and development towards autonomy, rather than a set of constructed norms designed to measure her or him against other children. It offers possibilities for careful, meaningful observation, identification and assessment of learning needs leading to more effective addressing and answering of those needs. It encourages the development of self-esteem and confidence and can even be seen as having the potential to prevent SEN from arising by providing the positive early experience necessary for full growth and development (Lloyd, 1994).

High-quality, effective early years education can clearly be seen, then, to provide a vitally important foundation stone for the whole of education, for all children. An education system which built upon this firm foundation and used its principles as a model to underpin the policy, provision and organisation of further levels to develop a genuinely inclusive education for all, clearly would offer real access to educational opportunity to all as an entitlement.

The 1988 Education Act enshrined in legislation, for the first time, exactly that entitlement. However, it is clear to those working in the early years of education and in SEN, that the measures imposed by the Act and much subsequent legislation, which purport to ensure that entitlement, have in fact resulted in enormous and rapid change, and a great deal of pressure. This, far from enabling more access to all children to an equal educational opportunity, can be seen to have the potential to impede it and lead to more exclusion. This discussion leads very clearly into consideration of the second major theme, identified at the beginning of this chapter: the influence of changes in education, especially in the curriculum, on early years education.

The effect on early years education of recent curriculum change

The 1988 Education Act introduced the National Curriculum as an entitlement curriculum, offering the means to ensure a broad, balanced education for all children. There are many, however, who dispute this claim and see the National Curriculum as narrowly prescriptive, instrumental in its aims and at best relevant and appropriate for a very small minority of children (Kelly, 1990; Lawton, 1989; White, 1988). Certainly the heavily traditional academic subject-base, the linear model of progression and the standardised age-related assessment procedures, make it difficult, if not impossible, to offer an inclusive educational opportunity for all, as discussed in the previous section.

Its influence on the early years can also be seen as increasingly worrying, for it has begun to have consequences for the way in which that phase of education is perceived, provided and practised. There is growing argument, particularly from politicians, that early years education should be regarded as the foundation and preparation for the National Curriculum and should therefore become a period of initiation into its procedures and practices. Gammage finds this particularly worrying:

> What frightens me more than the delusion that a centrally defined curriculum can be imposed on all children is the new and rather dangerous tendency to let *that* curriculum press down upon the provision for even the youngest children . . . It is here that many anxieties really begin to develop. Basically the argument beginning to be heard from politicians is that since they are becoming more and more convinced that early education matters, then it should be a version of that which they deem appropriate for older children.
>
> (Gammage, 1992:3)

For him, and indeed for many others working and writing in education (Blenkin and Kelly, 1994; Hurst, 1991, 1994; Lloyd, 1994), the National Curriculum, with its prescriptive academic subject-base, does not provide that balance, nor is it underpinned by a model which values individual growth and development and allows for children to play, explore, inquire and experience according to their individual needs.

Perhaps the most worrying feature of the downward pressure of the National Curriculum on early years education is the assessment procedures it employs to measure success and achievement. Standardised, norm-related testing, designed to compare children's progress with that of other children of the same age, is clearly opposed to the notion of differentiated rates and paces of development and to valuing diversity and difference – principles central to both early years education and to inclusion for children with SEN. Indeed the assessment procedures of the National Curriculum can be seen to be both élitist and exclusive:

> In the current educational climate, with its constant emphasis on testing and raising academic standards, there is a real danger that other qualities will be excluded, or at least undervalued. The narrow view being promoted of assessment as standardised testing of children's ability to read, write and cope with numbers, is potentially a process for expanding the number of children we brand as failures.
>
> (Lloyd, 1994:192)

Standardised assessment also has another very worrying role in current education policy – that of comparison. For the very young, and especially for those with SEN this raises many problematic issues. Gammage suggests we have a duty, in fact, to:

> . . . defend children from the gross and improper view that comparisons with others (and the possibly associated notion failure) are important elements in any worthwhile curriculum.
>
> (Gammage, 1992:5)

It is extremely worrying, therefore, that the recent guidelines produced for early years education (SCAA, 1996) are framed in terms of aims and objectives which are instrumental rather than developmental. The guidelines specify attainment targets to be reached by certain ages and assessment procedures used to measure achievement against narrowly conceived norms. It is equally worrying to note that the guidelines barely make reference at all to SEN.

Blenkin (1994) sees these approaches as totally incompatible with the principles of early years education discussed earlier:

> The National Curriculum is not just a different curriculum from the traditional early years curriculum; it is the mirror image, its exact opposite in every respect.
>
> (Blenkin, 1994:40)

She points to the enormous pressures on those working in the area who are currently trying to adhere to what they believe to be the essential principles of effective, high-quality early years education. At the same time they have to deal with the tensions created by the inappropriate model of the National Curriculum being forced down upon them.

For children identified as having SEN these changes and pressures can only prove to be counter-productive. Inevitably, the introduction of age-related attainment targets and a curriculum designed to produce conformity rather than to value diversity, can only lead to a narrowing of possibilities for genuine inclusion. At the same time there is the possibility that early years education itself, founded upon these very different principles, rather than the traditional principles discussed earlier, can create more SEN rather than provide the good start necessary to ensure that these needs do not arise.

Thus current pressure on early years education to change and conform to the principles underlying the National Curriculum and its assessment procedures, can be seen to be of extreme concern for all children, and particularly so for those identified as having SEN, who are perceived as being especially vulnerable at this crucial first phase of education.

Conclusions

Looking back to the principles of early years education, discussed earlier in this chapter, the issues raised above can be seen to give rise to considerable concern. Current pressures seem to be directed clearly towards bringing this all-important phase of education into line with those which follow it, rather than taking its traditional principles as the basis for future development in the later phases. The implications of this for children with SEN are indeed worrying.

This chapter highlights the importance of early years education for those children identified as having SEN, both in providing an inclusive and beneficial start in their education, and as offering a model for genuine inclusion in education. It has been argued that these are vitally important issues in the whole process of ensuring that all children, irrespective of ability, are to be ensured access to a genuinely equal educational opportunity, to which they are entitled. Early years education has an important part to play in ensuring that the entitlement is more than mere rhetoric. For that door to remain open for children with SEN, there is a need for colleagues working in the whole of education to recognise, and to make the case for, the retention of high-quality early years education which is founded upon:

- its traditional principles
- sound understanding of the principles of child development
- careful attention to the processes of learning
- provision of the necessary high-quality social interaction
- the need for opportunities for creative and imaginative development.

There is also a need to articulate the incompatibility with these principles of the current model which underpins the National Curriculum and its assessment procedures, which is being pressed down with such vigour upon the early years.

References

Barton, L. (ed.) (1989) *Integration, Myth or Reality*. Lewes: Falmer Press.

Barton, L. and Landeman, M. (1993) 'The politics of integration; observations on the Warnock Report'. In Slee, R. (ed.) *Is There a Desk With My Name on It? – The Politics of Integration*. Lewes: Falmer Press.

Blenkin, G. (1994) 'Early learning and a developmentally appropriate curriculum: some lessons from research'. In Blenkin, G. and Kelly, A. (eds) *The National Curriculum and Early Learning; An Evaluation*. London: Paul Chapman.

Blenkin, G. and Kelly, A. (eds) (1994) *The National Curriculum and Early Learning. An Evaluation*. London: Paul Chapman.

Bruce, T. (1987) *Early Childhood Education*. London: Hodder & Stoughton.

DES (1978) *The Report of the Committee of Enquiry into Handicapped People and Young Children* (The Warnock Report) London: HMSO.

DfEE (1994) *The Code of Practice for the Identification and Assessment of Special Educational Needs*. London: HMSO.

Gammage, P. (1992) *Standing Conference of Education and Training of Teachers, Occasional Paper 1. Quality: The Tension between Content and Process*. Nottingham: University of Nottingham.

Hurst, V. (1991) *Planning for Early Learning*. London: Paul Chapman.

Hurst, V. (1994) 'The Implications of the National Curriculum for Nursery Education'. In Blenkin, G. and Kelly, A. (eds) *The National Curriculum and Early Learning: An Evaluation*. London: Paul Chapman.

Kelly, A. (1990) *The National Curriculum – A Critical Review*. London: Paul Chapman.

Lawton, D. (1989) *Education Culture and the National Curriculum*. London: Hodder & Stoughton.

Lloyd, C. (1994) 'Special educational needs and the early years'. In Blenkin, G. and Kelly, A. (eds) *The National Curriculum and Early Learning: An Evaluation*. London: Paul Chapman.

Oliver, M. (1990) *The Politics of Disablement*. London: Macmillan.

Oliver, M. (1992) 'Intellectual Masturbation: A Rejoinder to Soder and Booth', *European Journal of Special Needs Education*, 7(1), 58–69.

Oliver, M. (1994) 'Does special Education have a Role to Play in the 21st Century?' Keynote Speech, St Patrick's College, Dublin.

Reiser, R. and Mason, M. (1990) *Disability Equality in the Classroom: A Human Rights Issue* (2nd edn.). Available from DEE, 78, Mildmay Grove, London N1 4PJ.

Slee, R. (ed.) (1995) *Is There a Desk With My Name on It? The Politics of Integration*. Lewes: Falmer Press.

Tomlinson, S, (1986) 'The expansion of special education'. In Cohen, A. and Cohen, L. (eds) *Special Educational Needs in the Ordinary School*. London: Harper and Row.

SCAA (1996) *Desirable Outcomes*. London: HMSO.

Wilson, J. and Cowell, B. (1986) 'How shall we define handicap?' In Cohen, A. and Cohen, L. (eds) *Special Educational Needs in the Ordinary School*. London: Harper and Row.

Index

Printed in the United Kingdom
by Lightning Source UK Ltd.
136079UK00001B/220/A